SENSATIONAL TV

Trash or Journalism?

—Issues in Focus—

Nancy Day

ENSLOW PUBLISHERS, INC.

44 Fadem Road	P.O. Box 38
Box 699	Aldershot
Springfield, N.J. 07081	Hants GU12 6BP
U.S.A.	U.K.

Library of Congress Cataloging-in-Publication Data

Day, Nancy.
    Sensational TV: trash or journalism? / Nancy Day.
        p. cm. — (Issues in focus)
    Includes bibliographical references and index.
    Summary: Questions whether the mass media, especially television, present an accurate
representation of the news or whether it is more concerned with the sensational story.
    ISBN 0-89490-733-6
    1. Sensationalism in television—Juvenile literature. 2. Magazine format television
programs—Juvenile literature. 3. Talk shows—Juvenile literature. 4. Reality television
programs—Juvenile literature. 5. Sensationalism in journalism—Juvenile literature.
[1. Television programs. 2. Talk shows. 3. Mass media.]
I. Title. II. Series: Issues in focus (Hillside, N.J.)
PN1992.8.S37D38 1996
791.45'653—dc20   95-35675
                                                CIP
                                                AC

Printed in the United States of America

10 9 8 7 6 5 4 3 2 1

Illustration Credits: America's Most Wanted, p. 72; NBC News, pp. 15, 33, 60;
Nancy Day, pp. 23, 64, 96; Payne-The Charlotte Observer, p. 39; "Rolonda" King
World Productions, p. 47 ; Vicki Abt, Pennsylvania State University, 1994, p. 53.

Cover Illustration: © Lannis Waters/The Palm Beach Post

Contents

The problem with television is that the people must sit and keep their eyes glued on a screen; the average American family hasn't time for it.

—a reviewer for *The New York Times* at a demonstration of a prototype television at the 1939 World's Fair.

Acknowledgments

I would like to thank Tom Colbert of Industry R&D; Steve Rendall of FAIR; Rolanda Watts and her staff; WTVI in Charlotte, North Carolina; Vicki Abt; John Walsh and the staff of "America's Most Wanted;" and NBC News for providing information, photographs, or other assistance. I also thank Robert and Betty Day for their advice and encouragement, and Joe Sakaduski for his continued love and support. And I thank Matt Sakaduski for being a remarkable person and a great buddy.

Author's Note

I was visiting my son's first-grade class when I noticed a little girl looking through a book about famous African-American women. The book contained exquisite photographs of well-known and important women from the arts, science, government, and other fields. As the little girl paged through pictures of women such as astronaut Mae Jemison, peace activist Coretta Scott King, and Congresswoman Shirley Chisholm, the teacher asked her if she recognized any of them. "No," she answered at first. "Well, there was one . . ."

As it turned out, the only prominent African-American woman that this seven-year-old African-American child could identify was Oprah Winfrey. Now I'm not saying that Oprah Winfrey isn't a talented, successful woman. Or that Oprah Winfrey isn't an acceptable role model. Or even that she shouldn't be admired and respected. But what does this say about who (or more accurately, what) is teaching today's children?

For a child to know so little about her own heritage specifically, and about American history in general (yet be able to immediately identify a talk show host) says a lot about where children are getting their knowledge these days. It also says a great deal about the role of television in our lives. The famous American journalist Edward R. Murrow called television the greatest classroom in the world. But what is it teaching? And, what is it *not* teaching?

I hate television. I hate it as much as peanuts. But I can't stop eating peanuts.

—Orson Welles [1]

1

The O.J. Saga

Over 90 million people watched—more than saw that year's Super Bowl. The white Bronco crawled along the highway, followed by a sea of police cars. It was hypnotizing. O.J. Simpson—football legend, movie star, advertising spokesperson, symbol of success—was inside, reportedly pointing a gun at his own head. He had been accused of the bloody murders of his wife and her friend. Could the American hero have done such a thing? People stayed glued to their television sets, eager to find out.

Coverage of the low-speed chase cost the three major television networks a total of between 6 and 8 million dollars. CBS reportedly lost one million dollars during the week of the pretrial hearing alone. [2]

Why all the attention? People were fascinated. They

couldn't get enough of it. And the networks felt that if they didn't give the people what they wanted, audiences would turn someplace else—most likely, the Cable News Network (CNN). CNN was a big winner anyway. For the week of July 4, 1994, CNN got forty-nine of the top fifty slots for highest-rated basic-cable programs.[3]

News programs scrambled to meet public demand. Every newsmagazine except "60 Minutes," which was in reruns, devoted at least one segment to the O.J. Simpson case. The pretrial hearings raised combined network ratings by more than 25 percent.[4] A clerk for the judge in the Simpson case estimated that in the first six months after the murders, there had been twenty-seven thousand newspaper and magazine stories on the case and that broadcast reports had been heard as far away as Tibet.[5]

Some critics complained that Simpson was being treated more like a respected hero than an accused murderer. They complained that film clips of Simpson scoring touchdowns were shown during the chase coverage, yet no mention was made of Simpson's 1989 flight from police responding to a frantic 911 call from his wife. Also, television coverage focused on Simpson and his legal strategy, not on his history of domestic violence.[6]

Other critics complained that when journalists fixate on a story like the Simpson case, they ignore other, more important issues. For example, during the "O.J. Summer," Richard Keil of Associated Press uncovered irregularities at the Resolution Trust Corporation, the federal agency in charge of the savings-and-loan bailout that reportedly cost taxpayers millions of dollars. And Timothy Aeppel, in a story on the front page of *The Wall Street Journal*, reported that cleanup work at seventeen key nuclear weapons plants and labs had uncovered uranium seeping into the groundwater—along with

8

other problems—which may cost hundreds of billions of dollars to fix. Yet neither of these stories received widespread coverage.[7]

In a weird way, major media events such as the O.J. Simpson case help draw people together. No one had to struggle to find a topic of conversation *that* week. Everyone, from the supermarket checkout clerk to the bank president, and from the corporate attorney to the kindergarten teacher, was talking about it. Did the news media do the right thing in responding to what they saw as public demand? Or did the media themselves fuel the frenzy by focusing too much attention on the case?

The public has always been interested in celebrities. People are curious about their private lives and are also eager to find proof that being rich and famous doesn't guarantee happiness. They like to see hypocrites exposed. The greater the fall from grace, the more people want to hear about it. But the O.J. Simpson case (and the media coverage of it) shows how news reporting has changed.

Some people say that TV has gone tabloid. They say that traditional journalism has been replaced by sensationalism. But sensationalism attracts viewers, viewers raise ratings, ratings draw advertisers, and advertisers write the checks that keep the networks in business. If viewers didn't watch sensational programs, the networks would dump them like last week's lasagna. But viewers *do* watch them. So the networks respond by producing more sensational programs. Producers say they are just giving viewers what they want. Is this true? And, if it is, what, if anything, should we do about it?

Real or Imagined?

The focus on the O.J. Simpson story reached such a frenzy that, looking back, it's hard to believe the depths to which

9

television programs plunged, trying to dig up new and exclusive information. See if you can guess which of the following were actually featured on television programs, and which are make-believe:

1. A hair replacement specialist servicing Lyle Menendez (in jail on suspicion of murdering his parents), who claimed to have received inside information on O.J. from jail visits to his client.

2. A reenactment, using a white Bronco, a limousine, and an actor, to see whether someone could get from the murder scene to O.J.'s house and then to the airport within the given time.

3. A show featuring people who fell in love while watching the Bronco being chased by police.

4. Women who worked on O.J.'s exercise video.

5. The "O.J. Stress Syndrome" (stress symptoms suffered by people who watched too much press coverage).

6. The real estate agent who sold O.J. his house.

7. People who look like O.J. and Nicole.

8. The man who sold O.J. shoelaces for the shoes he was wearing the night of the murder.

9. A woman who had lunch with O.J. seven years ago.

10. A poll on how people feel the O.J. Simpson case has affected their lives.

Numbers 1, 2, 4, 5, 6, 7, 9, and 10 were actually featured on television shows. Only numbers 3 and 8 are imagined—as far as I know.

Television is now so desperately hungry for material that they're scraping the top of the barrel.

—Gore Vidal [1]

2

McNews—The Dumbing of America

There can be no doubt that television plays a major role in the lives of most Americans. On average, Americans devote 40 percent of their free time to watching television and have the television on seven hours a day.[2] People watch television to be entertained, to relax, to escape, to avoid being lonely, and to find information—news.

But people raised on fast food want news that requires only small bites, is easily digested, and can be absorbed quickly. And as the nuggets of information have become smaller and the chunks of entertainment have become larger, the amount of information that television provides and the way in which it is provided have changed. There is also a trend toward what CBS Evening News anchor Dan Rather calls the "Hollywoodization" of the news, in which there is

11

greater interest in "the personalities, the celebrities . . . and the atmospherics than the substance."[3]

News vs. Entertainment

"World's First Head Implant," "Girl finds box of human eyeballs," "Alien Tombs Found in Washington," "Commuter found severed head on the way to work."

Welcome to the world of the tabloids.

Tabloids are the newspaper-style magazines in the check-out lane at the supermarket. They are filled with medical miracles, amazing diets, incredible crime stories, celebrity scandals, and alien encounters. Few people admit to reading the tabloids, but somebody must be reading them. Tabloid magazine sales are in the millions.

The success of the print tabloids has led to a television version—tabloid TV. There is no strict definition of what makes a television program tabloid. Some people use the same test that one Supreme Court justice used to identify pornography. He said he knew it when he saw it. Producers of programs labeled tabloid reject the term. They consider their shows newsmagazines, not tabloids. Most critics say that the content is what counts, not the label. They use the word tabloid to describe programs that consistently feature sensational stories. Howard Kurtz, a media reporter for *The Washington Post,* defines tabloid stories as those dealing with crime, sex, disasters, accidents, and public fears.[4]

Then there are the talk shows. Oprah, Sally, Maury, Montel—you don't even need their last names to know who they are. They chat with drunks, punks, hunks, stalkers, hawkers, tattoo artists, body piercers, nudists, Buddhists, racists, rapists, skinheads, and witches. They cover a wide range of subjects, but gravitate toward stories with a sex, violence, or celebrity angle, just like the tabloids. Some deal with serious issues and others are pure entertainment.

Reality-based shows deal with crime, disasters, accidents, and general mayhem. Most of them show real-life police officers and emergency personnel in action. In many cases, they also use reenactments, which are dramatizations using actors or the people who were involved.

What tabloid television, talk shows, and reality-based programs have in common is that they are often lumped together under the heading "trash TV." The term reflects a value judgment that some people argue is unfair. They do deal with serious subjects, but they do it differently than mainstream news programs. Or do they?

Newsmagazine shows such as "60 Minutes," "48 Hours," and "20/20" have begun covering the same juicy stories as the so-called tabloid shows such as "Hard Copy" and "A Current Affair." Even network news programs have increased their coverage of entertainment news and broadened their reporting of sensational news stories, arguing that they are simply giving the viewers what they want.

The public's appetite for sensationalism affects both how stories are selected and the coverage they receive. For example, the fact that Lorena Bobbitt cut off her husband's penis is of little consequence when compared to the problems facing our world; however, the Bobbitt case received substantial coverage by all of the news media. According to Richard M. Smith, editor-in-chief and president of *Newsweek*, television now sets the agenda for what the print press follows up on. The Bobbitt story and others like it "clearly would have been covered in the print press," says Smith, "but with the tabs in all their print and television forms throwing fuel on the fire, the more traditional press felt obliged to respond to what their readers and viewers were talking about over the dinner tables."[5]

Journalism or Sensationalism?

What is sensationalism? It can be the stories themselves that are sensational, the emotional way in which they are presented, or the emphasis on entertainment value. Sometimes sensationalism is simply defined as excess. George Juergens, in the introduction to his book on newspaper publisher Joseph Pulitzer, described the three dimensions of sensationalism as an emphasis on personalities, a preference for trivial over significant news, and the use of colloquial, personal language.[6]

The blurring of the line between journalism and sensationalism worries many people. What is missing, they say, is judgment about what is newsworthy and what is just nosy. Tragic events may be newsworthy (the assassination of a president) or carry a message (a drunk-driving crash), but sometimes there is no larger issue (an interview with a man who lost his wife in a plane crash). These stories serve no purpose except to capitalize on someone's tragedy.[7]

Some journalists say that you can't blame the messenger for the news. They say they report violence because we live in a violent society. As Joseph Pulitzer wrote:

> The complaint of the 'low moral tone of the press' is common but very unjust. A newspaper relates the events of the day. It does not manufacture its record of corruptions and crimes, but tells of them as they occur. If it failed to do so it would be an unfaithful chronicler. . . . Let those who are startled by it blame the people who are before the mirror, and not the mirror, which only reflects their features and actions.[8]

14

Journalists can help the public understand world events by providing in-depth coverage and analysis.

The twentieth edition of the Television Code (1978), formulated by the National Association of Broadcasters, includes a section titled "Treatment of News and Public Events." It addresses the issue of sensationalism in this way:

Good taste should prevail in the selection and handling of news. Morbid, sensational or alarming details, not essential to the factual report, especially in connection with stories of crime or sex, should be avoided. News should be telecast in such a manner as to avoid panic and unnecessary alarm.[9]

Today, it is hard to find evidence that good taste prevails. When the Bobbitt story surfaced, instead of hearing in-depth reporting on the subject of domestic violence, we were treated to news reporters across the country jumping all over each other, eager to use the word penis on the air. Through suppressed giggles, they told us every detail. We heard that Lorena Bobbitt was a manicurist. We were told about her husband's sexual habits. We saw the knife, heard how she did it, and were shown where she threw the discarded member. So much for avoiding "morbid, sensational or alarming details, not essential to the factual report, especially in connection with stories of crime or sex." It was exactly this story's combination of crime and sex that made it so irresistible.

But what *is* good journalism? Is it the simple reporting of bare-bones facts and figures or does it include the personal side of the news? Is the story the Los Angeles earthquake, or is it the dramatic rescue of a single man, trapped in his crushed car? Can news reporting really be objective? Should it be?

Herbert Gans, in his book *Deciding What's News,* discusses the media's built-in bias, its power to determine what is newsworthy, its interest in stories that are cheaply reported, and its focus on events that can be reported in dramatic ways. The stories that are chosen, the words used to describe events, and the ways in which stories are reported all affect the audience's interpretation of the information.[10] For these reasons, there can be no such thing as unbiased, unemotional journalism. This is particularly true when stories are glossed over quickly, and the audience is not given enough information to be able to understand and make judgments on the issues involved.

USA Today debuted in the early 1980s as a national daily newspaper specifically designed to give readers the kind of news that research showed they wanted. But criticism was swift and sharp. Hodding Carter, in his PBS press critique, called it "Mac-News," or fast food journalism.[11] Its format, designed for an audience used to television's "sound bites" or short snippets of memorable information, seemed to be a scaled down version of the news—a sort of prechewed meal of entertainment, interesting stories, and yes, news.

Today's television news reporting is receiving the same sort of critical reviews. Some people think we have lost track of what's important. They say we care more about what a certain celebrity had for lunch than we do about a child dying of starvation in India. Has news reporting deteriorated to the point that we have lost the ability to separate substantial from superficial, reality from fantasy, and essential from sensational? And if we have, when and how did it happen? Even more important, do we want to change it?

Have Things Really Changed?

Some say that broadcasting began when Stentor, the herald, rallied the Greeks before the gates of Troy. According to the ancient Greek poet Homer, Stentor had a good announcer's voice and "broadcast" to the besieging forces through a great horn.[12]

In ancient Rome, scribes described Senate proceedings and proclamations in *Acta Diurna,* the official court publication. They began to include news of births, deaths, marriages, and divorces. Unofficial newsletters sprang up to compete with the *Acta.* These newsletters described natural disasters, scandals, and changing alliances among noblemen—and so, were probably the first tabloids in world history.

Almost as soon as the printing press was invented in the mid-1400s, printed material began to spread across Europe.

17

From the sixteenth century through the eighteenth century, almanacs were the most popular reading material in England. They covered astrology, witchcraft, rapes, and hangings. Almanacs were also popular in France, where they included stories of amazingly long lives and monstrous births.

Sensationalistic news reporting was not limited to Europe. An issue of the first American newspaper, *Publick Occurences Both Foreign and Domestick,* published in Boston in 1695, contained accounts of suicide, the sexual escapades of members of the French Court, and an Indian massacre. In 1704, John Campbell founded the *Boston News-Letter,* the first successful American newspaper. In this paper, he included stories about storms, fires, drownings, Indian attacks, weird animals, and hangings.[13]

Not only is sensationalism in news reporting not new, criticism of news reporting is not new either. Thomas Jefferson suggested that editors divide their newspapers into four sections: Truths, Probabilities, Possibilities, and Lies.[14] Fisher Ames, a conservative American politician, wrote in 1801 "There seems to be a sort of rivalship among printers, who shall have the most wonders, and the strangest and most horrible crimes."[15]

The Age of Broadcasting

The first news ever heard over the air was the 1898 wireless (radio) coverage of a yacht race. Then, in 1909, Charles "Doc" Harrold began broadcasting regularly scheduled news reports and music from the Garden City Bank Building in San Jose, California.[16]

The first really big event broadcast on radio was the first solo, nonstop flight across the Atlantic Ocean. Charles Lindbergh took off from Roosevelt Field, Long Island, on May 20,

1927, at 7:52 A.M. in his single-engine plane, *The Spirit of St. Louis.* As an anxious world waited, word finally came by radio: "This is Station 2RF, Dublin, calling. The American flier Lindbergh passed over Dingle Bay on the Irish coast at a low altitude at 1:30 this afternoon." Within minutes there were cheers across America. Newspapers printed the full story, but people already knew the important part. He had made it. The power and immediacy of broadcast news reporting was clear.[17]

In 1932, Lindbergh was in the news again. This time at the center of a much sadder and more sensational story. His young son had been kidnapped. The story was reported in much the same way a celebrity tragedy would be today. People heard the smallest details about the baby being put to bed and how he was later discovered missing. The ladder up to the nursery window and footprints in the soft ground were discussed at length. Then the baby's body was found. People listened with fascination as radio broadcasters reported the arrest, trial, and execution of Bruno Richard Hauptmann.

The Lindbergh broadcasts generated such interest that Gabriel Heatter, the reporter who did three broadcasts a day from the courtroom, became a celebrity himself. In his autobiography, Heatter described the experience:

> I realized that radio had never before broadcast a murder trial and that this was the most sensational of all trials. I began to see Colonel Lindbergh's face on the keys of my typewriter. I seemed to feel him talking straight at me and saying, "Remember, this is a story of a dead baby. My baby." This was no time to sensationalize.[18]

Yet it was the sensational details the public wanted.

Another development that revolutionized news reporting was cable television. It started in the late 1940s in rural communities in Pennsylvania and Oregon, where mountains interfered with over-the-air reception. At first, news reporting was primitive. Local cable companies simply rolled typed-up stories in front of a camera. Gradually, cable broadcasting became more sophisticated and more widespread. Then, in 1980, Ted Turner founded CNN. News was now broadcast around the clock.

How News Reporting Has Changed

The Declaration of Independence was signed on July 4, 1776, in Philadelphia. The event was reported two days later in Philadelphia and six days later in New York. It took two weeks for word to reach Boston.[19] Almost two hundred years later, on November 22, 1963, President John F. Kennedy was shot while riding in an open limousine. A reporter in Kennedy's motorcade heard the shots, grabbed a radio-telephone, and within minutes the message "Three shots were fired at President Kennedy's motorcade today in downtown Dallas" was broadcast via teletype.[20] News of the shooting reached an estimated 62 percent of the American public within thirty minutes, and 90 percent within the hour.[21]

The technology available to news reporters today has fundamentally changed news coverage. Satellites allow broadcasts to be transmitted around the world. Cellular phones, laptop computers, fax machines, and other technologies provide faster response and better coverage of breaking stories. When a plane carrying CBS News associate producer David Hawthorne aborted takeoff and crashed into the water, Hawthorne helped several women get their children out on the wing of the plane. Then he climbed back into the plane, got his cellular phone, and called CBS. He was put on the air with Dan Rather for the first live report from the scene.[22]

The negative side of this immediacy is that people have come to expect instant news. Even though solid reporting takes time and requires in-depth research and analysis, the public now demands immediate coverage, regardless of how superficial it may be. This attitude has contributed to the growth of tabloid television.

Small, portable video cameras enable on-the-scene reporting by amateurs as well as professionals. On October 17, 1989, Debbie Kelly was driving across the San Francisco Bay Bridge when a major earthquake struck. She grabbed her video camera just in time to videotape a car plunging off the collapsed section of the bridge. The scene was replayed thousands of times across the country by hundreds of television stations. George Holliday's videotape of the beating of Rodney King by Los Angeles police officers played a major role not only in the reporting of the event, but also in the outcome of the eventual court cases. Citizen involvement in news coverage has increased not only the breadth but the intimacy of reporting. Ordinary people with cameras have allowed access to events that, in the past, would not have been captured by the news media.

The number and types of television news programs have changed. In 1984, there were only two newsmagazines and an early form of a reality-based show, "Ripley's Believe It or Not," on prime-time television. Now, viewers can choose from numerous newsmagazines, hours of reality-based programming, and countless made-for-TV movies based on true stories. In addition, the networks and cable news stations provide coverage of sensational events, and hours and hours of talk shows.

Television is a powerful medium for news reporting. It provides vivid images, immediate coverage, and access to events around the world. Television's ability to instantly reach and teach the public is unmatched. Political commentator George Will warned Hedrick Smith, a *New York Times* correspondent turned public broadcasting correspondent, that television is so much more powerful than print that "you are going to find that operating as a television reporter is like writing with a two thousand-pound pencil."[23]

What is News?

Every hour of every day, decisions are made as to what is news and what isn't. These decisions make the difference between what we hear about and what we don't. Some of the criticisms of news reporting center on this issue of what the news media choose to cover. Is a severed head found in the subway news? What about a hair found in a celebrity's salad? Is a homeless woman stealing a coat news? How about a movie star shoplifting a bag of peanuts? Which should get more coverage—an earthquake in Iran that killed twenty thousand people, or a child trapped in a well in Texas? Cultural prejudices often influence the decision. Most Americans would be more interested in the child in a well in Texas than a bunch of foreigners in a country many of us couldn't find on a map. So media attention will focus on the single child over the twenty thousand faceless casualties. But if that child in the well is Mexican, perhaps an illegal alien, the media's interest drops. Why? Because the majority culture values "foreigners" (anyone different from themselves) less than members of the mainstream white society. This same bias can be seen in crime reporting. Black-on-black crime, particularly in poor areas, receives little coverage. But if that same black perpetrator chooses a white victim, it makes a big splash. This fuels cultural prejudice and alters the public's perception of

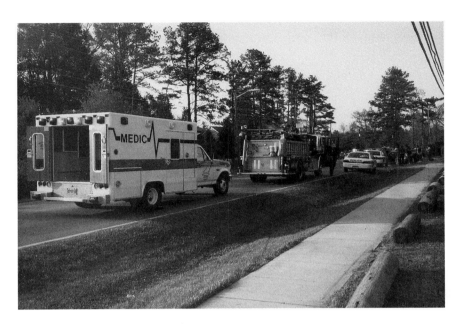

Dramatic pictures can make a story seem newsworthy.

reality. People are misled because they assume that if the media treat something as important, it must be important; if the media often talk about something, then it must be happening often. Not necessarily. In fact, some of the most important issues facing the world today (overpopulation, the environment, health issues) receive little attention, while some of the least consequential (whether O.J. did it or not, celebrity marriages and divorces, private lives of government figures) receive massive coverage.

Sometimes the decision of what to cover is as simple as which story has better pictures. An apartment house fire is more interesting to look at than a school board meeting. How do you *show* economic issues? How visual is an agriculture report? What do you put on the screen as a reporter talks about a new mathematical theory? As news anchor Dan Rather put it, "You can't take a picture of an idea."[24] But should visual appeal determine what is newsworthy?

A number of people have tried to answer the question "What is news?" Their answers show that the definition depends upon whom you ask:

When a dog bites a man, that is not news, but when a man bites a dog, that is news.

—Leo Rosten, political scientist and author

Anything that makes the reader say, "Gee Whiz!"

—Arthur McEwen, *San Francisco Examiner*
editorial writer

One Englishman is a story. Ten Frenchmen is a story. One hundred Germans is a story. And nothing ever happens in Chile.

—From a memo in the Fleet Street newsroom of a
British press lord

What somebody somewhere wants to suppress. All the rest is advertising.

—Lord Northcliffe, owner of the *Times* of London

Good news isn't news. Bad news is news.

—Henry Luce, founder of *Time*

News is the exceptional, something which threatens, benefits, outrages, enlightens, titillates or amuses.

—Mort Rosenblum, special correspondent for the
Associated Press

A dogfight in Brooklyn is bigger than a revolution in China.

—*Brooklyn Eagle* (no longer in existence)

Hey, Martha, take the meat loaf out of the oven and look at this.

—Arthur Lord, NBC[25]

*Our liberty depends on the freedom of the press, and that cannot be
limited without being lost.*

—Thomas Jefferson [1]

3

Newsmagazines
and Tabloids

The use of the word tabloid with journalism dates from the turn
of the century. Initially referring to a medicine or chemical in
tablet form, tabloid began to mean anything given or taken in a
compressed or condensed form—including news.[2] Tabloid TV
tends to bypass larger political and economic issues in favor of
dramatic, emotional tales. The term tabloid television has been
used as an insult applied to any type of news program that is
superficial or sensational in style. No one wants to be labeled
tabloid, but everyone is quick to pin the label on someone else.
Landon Y. Jones, managing editor of *People* magazine, calls the
syndicated tabloid shows the "crash dummies" of journalism.[3]

The Original Tabloids
The ancestors of today's tabloid television shows were the
news and ballad books of the 1600s. They often contained an

underlying moral or warning, and they covered "sad accidents," miracle cures, amazing survivals, royal weddings, murders (described in graphic detail), and bizarre births. And even three hundred years ago, critics complained about the unwholesome interest in sensationalism.

In the 1830s, the penny press (newspapers that were cheap and appealed to the masses) grew and, with it, a craving for sensationalism. Benjamin H. Day's *New York Sun*, James Gordon Bennett's *Herald*, and other penny press papers targeted the growing number of city residents whose reading skills were minimal. Stories were broken up into small, easy-to-read sections that contained vivid words and common slang. The moralistic tone remained, however, and so did the sensationalism. Take for example this pleasant little verse from a ballad on the murder of "Mr. May" in 1836:

> A frightful sight the body was, when found upon the road—His head all beat to pieces, and weltering in his blood; His teeth knocked from their sockets, were strewed all around, And clots of Mr May's life-blood was trodden in the ground.[4]

By the 1880s, improved technology allowed newspapers to use more illustrations. The audience of barely literate people eager for news expanded. When Joseph Pulitzer bought the *New York World* in 1883, he began the movement that became known as yellow journalism. He dropped the price of the paper and vowed to concentrate on "what is original, distinctive, dramatic, romantic, thrilling, unique, curious, quaint, humorous, odd, [and] apt to be talked about."[5]

By 1886, the *World's* 250,000 daily circulation was the largest ever. Imitators followed, most notably William Randolph Hearst with the *San Francisco Examiner*. Increasing competition led to even more bizarre and titillating stories. Hearst's editor, Arthur McEwen, defined the essential element of journalism as "the gee-whiz emotion."[6]

The first successful tabloid picture paper was *The New York Daily News,* established on June 26, 1919. As tabloids grew in popularity, they faced increasing criticism. In *The Independent,* S.T. Moore described tabloids as "an unholy blot on the fourth estate—they carry all the news that isn't fit to print."[7]

Thus began a tradition of gruesome pictures and outrageous stories that, at times, were totally inaccurate. *The New York Evening Graphic* used a composograph to add interest to a story about the Kip Rhinelander divorce in 1926. (A composograph is two photographs superimposed on each other to look like a single picture.) At the trial, Rhinelander's wife stripped to the waist in the courtroom. To report this sensational part of the story, the *Graphic* set up a courtroom using their own reporters as actors. A young woman, posing as Rhinelander's wife, was shown from the back. The paper later created a composograph by superimposing the heads of the actual court participants on the bodies of the reporters. The practice of altering reality continues today. Critics say print tabloids routinely fake photographs and that tabloid television programs often embellish the truth for the sake of a better story.

When Generoso Pope bought the *National Enquirer* in 1952, it had a circulation of seven thousand and contained mainly crime stories and racing tips. After some consideration, he decided to focus on gore. "I noticed how auto accidents drew crowds," he is quoted as saying, "and I decided that if it was blood that interested people, I'd give it to them."[8]

Today's tabloids concentrate on ironic twists of fate, ordinary people facing powerful forces or doing incredible things, celebrity scandals, and miracles of one kind or another. What hasn't changed is the conservative, moral undertone. Villains pay for their crimes, heroes are rewarded, people who revel in excess are punished. Religion, patriotism, and family values are good. Permissive parenting, big government, sexual misconduct, and feminism are bad. Minorities are seldom shown in a positive light. Women are encouraged to lose weight, find a mate, and have babies in order to be successful. If all else fails, the tabloids tell us, miracles happen.[9]

Newsmagazines

The first popular broadcast magazine was "March of Time" created for radio in 1931. During World War II, broadcast magazines such as "The Army Hour" and "Report to the Nation" were developed to lift morale. Then, in 1951, "Omnibus" debuted on CBS. It included original drama as well as informational programming.

In 1968, "60 Minutes" premiered on CBS. It became the most widely viewed, most profitable news program in television history. Meticulous research and solid investigative journalism were the "60 Minutes" trademarks. Television critic Tom Shales once said that "60 Minutes" is basically "an adventure show about four globe-trotting guys who are all but licensed to kill (in the name of truth, justice, and the American way, of course)."[10] ABC's "20/20," which started in 1978, was designed to increase the tempo of news reporting. Initially, the reviews were grim. One critic referred to "20/20" as "the most ill-conceived hour of broadcast news ever seen on ABC, a shapeless hodgepodge that included an overblown expose on rabbit killing, a fear-mongering story on terrorism, and several pointless features, all presided over by two anchors whose thickly accented speech could barely be understood." Another critic simply wrote "Ick, ick, poo, poo!"[11] Then "20/20" hired Hugh Downs, made other adjustments, and put their focus on "Why would I watch this?" They highlighted rock stars and other celebrities. Ratings began to climb. "The Elvis Cover-Up," an investigative piece on Elvis's death, became the most-watched news program of 1979.

In 1977, CBS tried a spin-off of "60 Minutes" called "Who's Who," which profiled celebrities as well as unknowns. It did not survive. Don Hewitt, the executive producer of "60 Minutes," has said that for "Who's Who" to have succeeded, it would have had "to get a little bit tabloid," which CBS refused to do at the time.[12]

Then came the entertainment news series. In 1978, CBS created "People," produced by Time-Life, publishers of *People* magazine. Next was NBC's "Real People," which featured unknown but unusual people like the Wisconsin lawyer who claimed that he had once had more than one hundred thousand people stored in suspended animation, all of them an inch tall. "That's Incredible!," "Wide World of People," "Couples," and similar programs began to appear, and local stations imitated them, using local stories. Television had discovered that audiences wanted to know more about celebrities and about regular people who are offbeat or bizarre.

"Evening Magazine" began in 1976 in San Francisco and then later spread to other cities. Two years later came "PM Magazine," which included some locally produced segments giving the program a community feel. In 1981, "Entertainment Tonight" began to provide show business news five nights a week.

News programs used to be "loss leaders," programs that lost money but were put on the air as a public service. But newsmagazines have become moneymakers for the networks. Producing an hour of news costs about $500,000 while a typical half-hour situation comedy can cost 1 million dollars an episode. Programs that have high ratings and are cheap to produce are extremely profitable. "I don't care how much Diane Sawyer is making, she's not nearly as expensive as Burt Reynolds," explained David Bartlett of the Radio-Television News Directors Association.[13]

While their producers are quick to point out that they are *not* tabloids, newsmagazines have frequently received the same criticism as the tabloids. Lawrence Grossman, a former president of NBC News and PBS, says the network newsmagazines practice "a sob sister kind of journalism. It's mostly heartthrob, good guy/bad guy stories. What's missing is hardedged stories about the economy, housing, the environment or health care."[14]

Barbara Walters says "the big question is the balance and the taste. If you care tremendously about the stories, as we do, then you can do an occasional Lorena Bobbitt."[15] She says the key is to balance emotional shows with shows on more serious issues, such as children with cancer and nuclear radiation.

Tabloids Come to Television

It was a warm summer day in Fremont, Ohio. At the end of a dead-end street known as the town's lovers' lane, Gary Offenburg and a woman named Lynn were making love in Gary's pickup truck. Randy Powers, who lived in one of the houses on the road, spotted the pair and called the sheriff. Powers was told that the prosecutor's office would need evidence, so he videotaped them. As it turned out, both Gary and Lynn were married—to other people. Gary was charged with public indecency and disorderly conduct. In another time, the shame, $150 fine, $33 dollars in court costs, and a 30-day suspended sentence would have been enough punishment for an unfaithful husband. But now we have tabloid TV.

After paying Powers a reported $2,500, "A Current Affair" showed the videotape, and an estimated 17 million people saw Gary and Lynn having sex in the pickup truck. Gary Offenburg was grappling with his public humiliation, fear that he might lose his job, and the anger of his wife and children, when "A Current Affair" aired the videotape again. A little more than a month later, Gary went down into his basement, put a pump-action shotgun to his chest, and pulled the trigger.[16]

Was the story of one adulterous couple news? Did the public's right to know override the individual citizens' right to privacy? Do people, through their misdeeds, give up their privacy? How would you feel if one of them was *your* parent?

The use of stories about individuals to make information more accessible and interesting is not new. Individuals add authenticity and realism to discussions of broad issues. What bothers some people about tabloid television is that the larger context is ignored. For example, the Offenburg video was not shown within a discussion of marital infidelity or morality in today's culture. It was simply run as a curiosity—something the audience would enjoy seeing. Here were people caught doing something that, although common, is considered wrong. Television viewers could watch from their living rooms, passing judgment without knowing many of the details about the individuals involved, their family situations, their feelings about the relationship, etc.

Critics of tabloid television are concerned about the effects these shows are having. "There's no doubt that the tabs have made society grosser," says Louis Hodges, professor of journalistic ethics at Washington and Lee University.[17]

Entertainment news has begun to crowd out "hard" news stories. Although there are still non-tabloid options for serious news consumers, it is becoming increasingly hard to find news programs that can resist devoting major portions of their coverage to stories like the O.J. Simpson trial that so captivate the public that their thirst for details seems unquenchable.

Which are the Tabloids?

The success of tabloid television has not gone unnoticed by the mainstream media. In one week alone, the premier of ABC's "Turning Point" featured an interview with Charles Manson and two former members of his "family"; "Dateline NBC" showcased serial killer Jeffrey Dahmer and his father; CBS's "48 Hours" dealt with the case of Russell Obremski, convicted of two Oregon murders in 1969 and recently freed on parole; and NBC's "Now" featured a man in prison for kidnapping children and doing "unspeakable things" to them.[18]

It's hard to argue convincingly that these shows are all that different from the shows labeled as tabloids. So-called tabloid shows may tell us as much or more about the state of our society than many stories on mainstream news programs. Some say they could be considered a form of documentary journalism, revealing the struggles of real people trying to cope with today's world.[19] After all, news is storytelling. It involves heroes, villains, conflicts, and resolutions. And that's just what the tabloids are providing.

Bill O'Reilly, anchor of "Inside Edition," says that his show is more like a newsmagazine than a tabloid. When asked about paying for stories, he says that "the networks pay

Critics say that the media should focus on hard news. Here Bryant Gumbel interviews President Bill Clinton on the "Today" show.

consultants and freelancers. What's the difference?" O'Reilly says that only about 25 percent of what you see on "Inside Edition" deals with tabloid stars (people like the Bobbitts or Susan Smith—the woman convicted of killing her two children). While he admits "we're not *U.S. News & World Report*," he says that people in his business take themselves very seriously. And he thinks some of the newsmagazines could use a little more emotion.[20]

Mike Watkiss, the Los Angeles bureau chief for "A Current Affair," has a master's degree from Columbia University and has won awards on local stations in Salt Lake City. "We don't cover the water board," he says. "We go after stories of human drama that have heartbeat, passion. The fact is, the networks had lost their way, and now they're falling in behind us."[21]

Steve Rendall, senior analyst with FAIR (Fairness and Accuracy in reporting), a national media watch group, agrees that the so-called tabloid shows are no different from mainstream news programs—but not because the tabloids are becoming more respectable. "The *Enquirer*, and Geraldo, and Ted Koppel; they're all trying to do the same thing," says Rendall. "They're trying to deliver readers or viewers to sponsors." Rendall did a study of "Nightline" shows from January 1 to March 16 of 1994 and found that 9 percent of Ted Koppel's coverage in the first three months—a quarter of 1994—was on Tonya Harding (a professional ice skater accused of arranging to have competitor Nancy Kerrigan injured). "*That's* tabloid" says Rendall. And "that's 'Nightline,' one of the most prestigious shows in television news . . . nearly 10 percent of their coverage, in a time that was rich with all kinds of things happening."[22] Why all the coverage? Again, popular stories draw viewers, viewers draw advertisers, and advertisers pay money.

Tabloid TV does have its good points. *Time* magazine media reporter Richard Zoglin says, "their style may be cheesy and their tactics dicey (including liberal use of the checkbook), but they are doing a lot of old-fashioned, roll-up-your-sleeves journalism."[23] Investigative reporting plays a big part on many of these shows. They go after scam artists, corrupt businesses, and people who have escaped punishment for misdeeds. They doggedly pursue their targets until "they get answers or until they get the door slammed in their faces," according to an "Inside Edition" advertisement.

Viewers enjoy seeing crooks badgered by reporters and

unveiled for the weasels they are, and in the process, the viewers may learn not to be so gullible. Watching these reports can help people develop a "BS" detector that may prevent them from being victims of similar scams.

The shows also call attention to cases in which justice has not been served. The public outrage they stir up is sometimes enough to push authorities to take action. As Phil Donahue points out, "They may be the last best hope when the cops arrest your sister. It's a cinch the networks aren't going to try to get your sister out of jail."[24]

Political Agendas

It's easy to tell the bad guys from the good guys on tabloid shows. If they are not already in jail, we are told they should be. If they've gotten off too easily, we're made to feel angry. A woman on welfare is shown to be getting more money than a woman who is working to support her family. A woman who was assaulted is shown fighting to keep the perpetrator in prison. Hard-working, abused employees are suffering at the hands of an uncaring, profit-hungry corporation. If someone is accused, he or she must be guilty. There are no shades of gray and no room for questioning the accuracy or fairness of the picture painted.

Unlike reporters on traditional news programs, who attempt to be objective, tabloid reporters openly react and express opinions. Tabloid proponents say this shows that reporters are involved and that they care. Critics say the reports are biased and trivialized. "Politically, tabloid is cynical; morally it is conservative, if not righteous," says author Graham Knight. "Against the greed, corruption, self-interest, and indifference of the powerful, on the one hand, and the moral and physical danger and threat of the deviant, on the other, tabloid sets up the people as the bearers of ordinary virtues such as common sense, caring, decency, fairness, and responsibility."[25] Like comic book characters, there are no complexities. The victims have no faults, and the villains have no positive attributes.

Inherent in almost every tabloid program is a moral or a warning: don't get involved with drugs, don't leave your doors unlocked, protect your children, have faith. The bottom line is usually WATCH OUT—THIS COULD HAPPEN TO YOU.

Checkbook Journalism

Traditionally, mainstream news media have refused to pay interview subjects. The basis for this rule is that it encourages well-meaning people to embellish their stories in order to justify the money they receive. It might even cause not-so-well-meaning people to make up stories in order to get paid. Either way, it raises the question of whether a story that has been bought is as credible as the one given by someone who had nothing to gain. Some argue that if purchased information is used in a news report, viewers should be told it has been bought so they can weigh the value of it.

Tabloid television shows were not the first to pay for news. In the 1800s, a speaker of the House of Representatives earned a hundred dollars a week by charging reporters for interviews. *The New York Times* paid for Robert E. Peary's expedition to the North Pole in exchange for exclusive rights to his story.[26] In 1975, CBS paid H.R. Haldeman, Nixon's top White House aide, $100,000 for two televised interviews.[27]

Tabloid television programs have made paying sources routine. Krista Bradford, formerly of "A Current Affair," says that although the tabloid shows don't like to talk about how often they buy interviews or cooperation, they all have huge "war chests" (of money) for just that purpose. "Why else would many of these people talk to these programs?" she asks. It's not unusual now for people with stories to tell to demand payment from reporters before they talk. Sources are "coming out of the woodwork" according to someone at "Hard Copy," says Bradford.[28]

The main reason tabloids, and others, pay interview sources is to get exclusive rights. If they can prevent a source from talking to other news media by buying the rights to his or her story, they have created a product no one else can offer. This gives them something unique that will increase their audience, their ratings, and therefore, their income.

Unfortunately, the public suffers because the free flow of information has been restricted. Once the tabloids start spreading money around, says investigative reporter Harvey Levin of KCBS-TV in Los Angeles, "sources are no longer available to the mainstream media, who then proceed to throw rumors on the air without exercising quality control."[29] The mainstream press depends upon information from a variety of sources in order to produce an accurate picture of what has happened. Without free access to these sources, pieces of the story may be missing, and the audience may suffer by getting an incomplete, even misleading, report.

In some cases, the judicial process has been affected. A woman who claimed to have seen O.J. Simpson driving near the murder scene accepted $5,000 from "Hard Copy" and $2,600 from the *Star* for her story. As a result, the prosecutors in the Simpson case reportedly didn't seek her testimony in court because they feared it was tainted.

Is paying sources a bad practice? In some cases, money may encourage witnesses to come forward. This can uncover critical information needed by the police. Like bounties placed on outlaws, it may even lead to a criminal's capture. And, some argue, what is the difference between people who make money from interviews and those who profit later from books and movie deals?

Fascination with Celebrities

People love celebrities. They are curious about their possessions, their love lives, and most of all, their misdeeds. So what's the harm if people really do want to know what kind of underwear President Clinton wears or how many people Madonna has slept with? Inquiring minds want to *know.*

Being obsessed with celebrities reflects an interest in the superficial aspects of life—money, fame, sexual conquests—rather than the more serious concerns of love, commitment, and working to succeed. If people spend their time watching celebrities and dreaming of being rich and famous, they probably aren't pursuing the very things that might lead to their own success—education, training, and hard work. At the extreme, fascination with celebrities can even lead to stalking, says Mark Crispin Miller, professor of media studies at Johns Hopkins University.[30]

Due to the limited supply of real celebrities, overnight celebrities are replacing them, according to James Willwerth, a *Time* magazine correspondent. Real celebrities such as Michael Jackson and Madonna have given way to celebrities of the moment such as Lorena Bobbitt, Susan Smith, and Kato

Critics say talk shows try to outdo each other by finding guests who represent the extremes of society.

Kaelin (O.J.'s former house guest who gained fame through his participation in the trial).

In the past, a person usually had to accomplish something to get media attention. Now, ordinary people in extraordinary circumstances become celebrities. However, interest in ordinary people is short-lived. Nancy Glass, anchor of the syndicated television program "American Journal," says that these ordinary celebrities have become "disposable," like tissues. This creates constant pressure to find new instant celebrities.[31]

The quickest way to become an instant celebrity is to commit a horrible crime. Newsmagazines and talk shows scramble to get exclusive interviews. Anyone who has ever had even the slightest connection with the criminal is brought out to tell us what we want to hear—that these people are animals and not like us at all.

Tabloid television shows continue to draw viewers, regardless of the criticism, and that is the key to success. As Linda Ellman, former co-executive producer of "Hard Copy" says, "the reason this kind of story [is] on the air is there is an appetite for it."[32]

Television is an invention that permits you to be entertained in your living room by people you wouldn't have in your home.

—David Frost [1]

4

The Talk Shows

The topics range from makeup tips to "the case of a twelve-year-old girl who was tortured and burned alive by teen girls," and from "teens arrested for being intimate on a bed in a department store" to "current Alzheimer's disease research." The usual format is that several people share their stories, experts give advice, and audience members offer their own opinions. Some shows make an effort to promote serious discussion on important issues; others make an effort to create confrontation in order to entertain.

Talk Show Guests

You've seen them. Ordinary people leading desperate lives filled with bad luck and worse judgment. Extraordinary people leading outrageous lives filled with unconventional actions and no judgment, sharing their most intimate problems, most painful personal tragedies, most irresponsible actions. Where do they come from? Why do they do it? Some are motivated by fame and fortune. In the 1950s, women who told the most sad and tragic stories about their hard lives won household appliances on "Queen for a Day" and similar shows. Today, talk show guests tell even more intimate and humiliating tales for less tangible rewards. Most talk shows do not pay guests for their appearances. Each guest gets a plane ticket, a night in a big-city hotel, and a chance to be (temporarily) a celebrity. Being able to tell their friends that they were on national television may be important to people who have no other way to gain recognition. Talk show guests may also have a vague hope that someone will want to make a movie of their story or that they will be "discovered" in some other way. Some critics say that these rewards, and hopes for rewards, can be enough to encourage guests to embellish their stories. At the very least, it seems to be enough to encourage them to give up their privacy.

Other guests are motivated by concern for themselves or others. They may hope that by coming forward with their painful experiences, they will help bring forbidden subjects out into the open, help people with similar problems deal with them, or help prevent people from having the problem in the first place. Additionally, confessing sins can be liberating. They may hope that by clearing their consciences they can also cleanse their souls and be able to move on with their lives. Some may feel they need advice and turn to talk shows for guidance. Appearing on a talk show may be the only way some people can get family members to confront their particular problem. These guests may feel that their appearance

42

will solve a problem they are unable to deal with in any other way.

University of Georgia researchers Patricia Joyner Priest and Joseph R. Dominick interviewed people who had appeared on "Donahue." They found that many of the guests represented "out-groups" (groups that are considered deviant by society or that are looked on with disapproval by others). This definition covers a wide range of groups, including people with AIDS, transsexuals, rape survivors, incest victims, gay parents, and prostitutes. These guests, say the researchers, had an almost evangelical desire to correct public perceptions about themselves. Their motivation was not fame, fortune, or even emotional release, but the desire to get people to see them as real people, not as stereotypes. Members of out-groups were willing to risk ridicule and criticism for a chance to communicate their message. The researchers found that these guests' appearances were a result of personal empowerment, not dysfunction.[2]

Being on television also gives guests a platform from which they can justify their behavior. Pennsylvania State University researcher and sociologist Vicki Abt points out that rather than being ashamed, guests eagerly discuss all sorts of immoral and even criminal behavior in an effort to seek understanding by others. Abt is concerned that the talk shows allow such guests the opportunity to promote the idea that they are victims of a disease, not just irresponsible, weak people.[3]

Critics also complain that talk shows reward people for bad behavior by giving them the opportunity to be on television. During the Los Angeles riots, for example, looters appeared on "Oprah!" Talk shows have featured child-abusers, wife-beaters, serial murderers, and people who have committed

43

other illegal acts. Although the shows' hosts defend this practice by saying that the audience can learn from it, more cynical observers wonder if it isn't concern for high ratings that is the real motivation.

The experts on talk shows are usually people who have written books they want to promote or who have businesses to publicize. But where do the regular guests come from? Many talk show participants come forward on their own. Most shows solicit participants during the show through short advertisements: "Do you want to confront a loved one about their dishonesty? Call 1-800 . . ." In any case, guests are not chosen because they represent a true sample of the world at large.

Talk shows may perform a public service by providing a forum in which people can discuss sensitive issues and be connected with resources such as support groups and associations that can help them. Seeing talk show guests admit they have problems may help some viewers realize that they themselves need help. At the very least, it lets them know that they are not alone. Sometimes, even the hosts come forward with startling admissions. During the taping of a program about recovering from drug addiction, Oprah Winfrey started to cry and admitted she had smoked cocaine in her early twenties.

Talk shows draw huge audiences, which gives them the opportunity to provide information to a large number of people. Some take this responsibility to heart and attempt to provide a larger context for the stories. Even though stories are often told through individuals, larger issues can be addressed. For example, a show on teachers who had affairs with students, while juicy, may actually address the problem of sexual harassment in our culture.

Some critics say that talk shows have become a substitute

for the Roman coliseum, in which wealthy patrons were entertained by watching people being devoured by lions. Today, a largely middle- and upper-class audience watches with amusement as lower-class guests fight over unfaithful lovers, deal with out-of-control teenagers, and feud with family members who have betrayed them in various ways. Communications professor Elayne Rapping points out that although talk show subjects seem frivolous, emotional, and on the fringes of society, they are almost always related in some way to deep cultural and structural problems in our society.[4]

Entertainment or Exploitation?

Some of the talk shows do not even pretend to deal with serious issues. Their subjects are usually specific people or situations, such as a man who had affairs with his wife's relatives, mothers who confront the men who have broken their daughters' hearts, women who are torn between two lovers, and so on. The audiences are encouraged to get involved, often behaving more like the crowd at a hockey game than the audience for a television program. For example, one episode of "The Richard Bey Show" featured two women who were fighting over the same man. As the host chatted with one of the women and the man onstage, the other woman was shown waiting offstage. The words "In hallway—can't see or hear!" flashed on the screen. Then the other woman was brought in from offstage and seated next to the first woman, inviting trouble. Sure enough, accusations were made, insults flew, and to the delight of the cheering crowd, a punch was thrown. Throughout the show, amusing voices saying things like "you're busted" when a man was

45

shown to have cheated on his mate made the tragedies of people's lives seem like just good fun.

Laughter is a common part of these shows—often at someone's expense. Guests who are not believed or who are seen as "bad guys" are howled at, jeered, and booed like the actors in the old melodramas. Women and children who have been victimized are the most popular heroes. Their tragic tales draw oohs and outrage. The hosts drag the most intimate details out, while holding the guests' hands, offering them tissues for their tears or patting them on the shoulder.

Even serious situations are treated lightly on some of the shows. "This pregnant woman has two lovers," read a teaser (a preview of what is coming up) during a "Jerry Springer" show. "Both think they are the father. Someone's in for a surprise! Stay tuned." Later, when the woman was onstage, Springer said "as the camera turns to you, tell us—who . . . is . . . the father . . . of your baby?" The woman then coyly unfolded a tee shirt with the father's name on it. The audience cheered. This light, quiz show approach makes for good entertainment, but should situations such as marital problems and unplanned pregnancies be treated in this way?

Some talk show hosts try to stay above the fray. Phil Donahue, for example, has tried to maintain a mix of hard-hitting informational shows and entertainment shows. Rolonda Watts, host of the "Rolonda" show, graduated from the prestigious Columbia School of Journalism. "First and foremost, I'm a journalist," she says. "What makes talk shows different are the hosts." The "Rolonda" show has tackled such issues as gun control, teen sexuality, welfare fraud, gay rights, and AIDS in the work place. Watts doesn't shy away from emotion, however. "I have the chance to make people feel something," she says. "What we're trying to do is empower

Rolonda Watts has addressed many tough subjects on "Rolonda." She wants her audience to *think* as well as *feel*.

them by examining issues that are relevant, thought-provoking and passionate."[5]

Talk Shows as Therapy

Some critics say that therapy as entertainment can be dangerous. They say that talk show hosts exploit guests when they promote the idea that talking (on television) helps with the healing process. Using the excuse that they need to educate and inform the audience, the hosts prod guests for ever more titillating details. "Phil, Sally and Oprah always know best," says Vicki Abt, who has done a study of talk shows. "They take the roles of caring parents, understanding friend, knowing therapist. They may not have professional credentials to give advice, but they do so freely."

Members of the audience tell guests to leave spouses, kick out misbehaving young people, and quit jobs, yet they bear no responsibility for the results of their advice. Hosts ask guests questions most people would never ask even their closest friends. The audience encourages the guests to open up and reveal all. Then we all listen in amazement as the guests do exactly that, on national television, with no chance to change their minds or to prevent friends, relatives, employers, and complete strangers from gaining access to the information.

The idea that therapy is a cure-all seems to be widespread on the talk shows. Some even allow psychologists to perform role-play exercises and other counseling techniques on stage. But, says Vicki Abt, the therapy provided by talk shows ignores the need for knowing a patient's history, only dealing with issues the person is ready to handle, tailoring therapy to the needs of the patient, providing follow-up, and granting the most basic element of responsible mental health care—privacy.[6]

For many people, talk shows are a primary source of information. Medical information, advice on relationships, and psychological terminology are tossed around in an informal way, which can create problems for people who rely on talk shows rather than on physicians or other experts who have access to information about the person's individual situation.

Responsible hosts are quick to point out to callers that they should see their own physicians or therapists for specific advice. Some ask the callers to hold so that staff members can put them in touch with the proper resources. Occasionally, the host or guest expert gets directly involved by talking off the air with a guest who seems to be in a particularly precarious situation. And some shows even try to stay in touch with past guests.

But what about therapy for the viewers? Some viewers tune in when the subject is relevant to them, and they may take away new knowledge or perspectives. Others watch for the simple reason that shows like these give them the comforting feeling that "at least my life isn't that bad." Maybe talk shows provide an escape from the boring lives many people lead. Or they may serve as a diversion from the urgent issues of the day. For these reasons, talk shows may help reduce stress and provide a sense of well-being among viewers, whether or not they benefit the participants.

Providing a Political Soapbox

In the old days, people would stand on overturned soapboxes, tree stumps, or whatever was available, and express their political beliefs to anyone who would listen. Today's soapbox is the talk show. People of almost any political opinion, no matter how extreme, can gain access to a platform that reaches millions of people. In fact, the more extreme the point of view, the more likely they will be welcomed as interesting and controversial guests. But by seeking out groups on the fringes of society, and having them face off against each other, talk shows may inadvertently be giving such groups not only visibility, but credibility. Who knew much about skinheads, for example, before talk shows provided a place for them to air their views?

Our culture values and protects freedom of speech and the ability to express conflicting opinions. We need to keep an open mind to all points of view. Yet some people worry about the exposure extremists are receiving. Even when guests offering opposing points of view share the stage, the situation implies each point of view has equal value. And factual errors made by talk show hosts, guests, and audience members are often not corrected, leaving the audience misinformed at best, misguided at worst.

Steve Rendall feels that extremists should be allowed to speak. "Our point isn't that these people should be kept off," says Rendall. "We should know about skinheads, we should know about Paul Hill [the man who defended the killing of abortion providers and later killed one himself]. It's just that their feet have to be held to the fire." Rendall says that interviewers should be tougher on such guests and should hold them accountable for their opinions.[7]

Talk show hosts often share their own feelings, unlike other journalists. Part of Oprah Winfrey's appeal is that she discusses her own experiences and feelings as they relate to the show's topic. Other hosts openly show their own political leanings or opinions. Geraldo Rivera, discussing O.J.

Simpson's sentence for beating his wife, called it "rinky-dink probation" and referred to the note found in Simpson's home as the "so-called suicide note." However, does being a talk-show host make an individual's opinion any more authoritative? And does the audience stop to ask what qualifications the hosts have for making judgments?

In her article "Daytime Inquiries," Elayne Rapping compares the talk shows to the women's consciousness-raising groups of the 1960s. But instead of empowering women, she says, the shows sap their political energy. "They are all talk and no action," according to Rapping. They allow women to voice their opinions, to argue, and to express emotion. They allow them to hear about approved services and institutions that might help with a particular problem. But women are not encouraged to actively work for change, says Rapping.[8] Rolonda Watts hopes that her show *does* compel people to work for change. She says "information is power" and says she hopes "to compel them in some way to take positive action of their own."[9]

Ethics and Responsibility

Can you imagine what it would be like to find out that you had a sister or brother you never knew about, or to meet the mother who gave you up for adoption when you were born? Picture being reunited. The fear. The emotion. The tears. Now imagine all this on national television, in front of a live audience.

Reunions have become popular on talk shows. Some reunite long-lost relatives in happy, tearful onstage meetings. Others confront cheating mates with people who claim to have slept with them or people who dispute their stories:

"This is Sidney. No one knows he is here today. Let's see what happens when Sidney confronts Olethia about their relationship." (He didn't know she was sleeping with her best friend's boyfriend.) This type of reunion is called an ambush. It is not quite as happy.

Sometimes, shows solicit guests by offering to reunite them with someone they can't find. Naturally, reunions are on-the-air, not private. For someone desperately trying to find a loved one, that may be a small price to pay. But is it really fair to the people involved?

Talk shows don't seem to discourage violence, and some even seem to encourage it. They pit feuding relatives against each other and provide a forum for opposing groups to confront each other. In a famous case, even the host got involved. During a taping of "Geraldo," a fight erupted among the guests. As cameras rolled, three grown men, including host Geraldo Rivera, clobbered and smashed each other. Rivera suffered a broken nose, later commenting "At least I got a couple of real good shots in." The show was later broadcast.[10]

Audience members seem to enjoy the confrontations. Jerry Springer's security guard sits in the front of the audience or even joins the guests on stage to control particularly volatile guests. People seem to like the excitement of the conflict. But is it healthy?

Reality seems to have been lost somewhere along the line. Do many families perform together as strippers? Have a lot of people had their identities stolen by imposters? How many women want their best friends to have their husbands' babies? Judging by the talk shows, these things are as common as tall people at a basketball game.

Researcher George Gerbner and his colleagues examined television's effect on viewers. They found that the media

Vicki Abt, Ph.D., of Pennsylvania State University, has studied talk shows and says that they may be affecting society's moral values.

create a mythology about women, minorities, crime, and so on, that shapes viewers' understanding and response to their real environment.[11] Gerbner and others have found that, if people watch a lot of television, the line separating the artificial world of television and the real world in which they live can become blurred. Are we losing the ability to tell what is real and what is not?

In their report on talk shows, Vicki Abt and fellow researcher Mel Seesholtz argue that a steady diet of bizarre and extreme behavior may chip away at society's moral boundaries, breaking down the wall between right and wrong. They studied twenty episodes each of "The Donahue Show," "The Sally Jessy Rafael Show," and "The Oprah Winfrey Show" and then published their findings. According to Abt:

> Cultural distinctions between public and private, credible and incredible witnesses, truth and falseness, good and evil, sickness and irresponsibility, normal and abnormal, therapy and exploitation, intimate and stranger, fragmentation and community are manipulated and erased for our distraction and entertainment.[12]

Talk shows are not interested in reflecting the real face of our society, she says, but in highlighting and trivializing its underbelly.

Have talk shows affected society's morals? Do we accept incest, adultery, deceit, bigotry, and other illegal or immoral behaviors more readily because we're used to hearing about them on talk shows? And what will be the result as the shows go to greater lengths to shock us by finding even more bizarre and abnormal situations to showcase?

A turning point for talk shows may have come in 1995 on a "Jenny Jones Show" with the theme "secret admirers." Jonathan Schmitz excitedly waited on stage, in front of television cameras and a live audience, to meet his mysterious admirer. Perhaps it would be the woman of his dreams. Then, out walked Scott Amedure, a gay man. Jonathan, wearing the new clothes he had bought for the occasion, was more than disappointed. He was humiliated. He was enraged. In the end, it appears, he became a murderer—and Scott Amedure was dead. Tom Shales, a staff writer for *The Washington Post*, was one of many critics who used the case to criticize the ambush technique that has become popular on many talk shows. The technique is used to provoke responses (anything from salty insults to flying fists) for the amusement of the audience. Unfortunately, Schmitz was not amused, and Amedure became a victim. "He died not for love but for ratings," said Shales of Amedure.[13]

Despite the shortcomings of talk shows, some people feel that they perform a valuable service. They say that frank discussions about difficult topics educate the public about important problems and encourage tolerance of different lifestyles. Issues such as eating disorders, child abuse, alcoholism, homosexuality, and domestic violence are now openly discussed, in part due to the tremendous visibility given by these shows. "Leeza," for example, featured children with facial deformities on a program called "Plastic Surgery Miracles." Such shows can help people understand the challenges others face. Phil Donahue has devoted many programs to educating people about AIDS. A "Ricki Lake" show about divorced fathers called "She Won't Let Me See My Kid" showed statistics about child custody, support, and visitation each time it went to a commercial.

Critics say that the talk shows are driven by a need for profits, not a desire to educate. Talk show host Phil Donahue admits that he is torn between wanting to cover important issues and having to get high ratings. "We get paid to draw a crowd," he says. "When we don't draw a crowd, we don't get paid." He complains that Peter Jennings can do a piece on date rape, but if a daytime talk show such as "Donahue" covers it, it's called trash TV.[14] He also cites the need to give audiences what they want. "They won't watch male strippers five days a week," says Donahue of talk show audiences, but "you'd better haul them out once in a while if you want to survive in the daytime arena. The audience appears to be largely interested in Madonna, not Managua."[15]

Proponents say that appearing on a talk show can be a life-changing experience. It can free people from the burden of carrying painful secrets and can help them deal with their problems. It allows people to tell their side of the story. The catharsis they undergo is healthy, say some. Viewers say they enjoy talk shows and learn from them. They say they are harmless and entertaining.

Male genitals found on railroad track. Stay tuned to the eleven o'clock news for details.

—News teaser during prime time on KGO-TV, San Francisco[1]

Sex, Violence, and Politics

From time to time, there is a public outcry to DO SOMETHING about all the sex and violence on television. Yet, the public seems to enjoy watching sex and violence. If they didn't, the shows would have no audiences. Then there is that troubling First Amendment to the Constitution that protects freedom of speech and freedom of the press. Should television programs be censored? Or are the media just giving us what we want?

Meeting a Need

It was a perfect example of our craving for sensationalism: "Everyone even remotely connected with the case was interviewed, trailed and hounded. . . .The newspapers pawed and sifted every aspect of the case. . . . Rude cartoons and lurid pamphlets exploited the scandal mercilessly. . . . Political and social leaders fought for tickets [to the trial]"[2] The O.J. Simpson case? The Bobbitts? Susan Smith? No. You have to go back over one hundred years to the 1870s. Henry Ward Beecher, a nationally famous and respected minister, had been having sex with a friend's wife for years. When he was sued by the husband, the publicity created a demand for juicy details that sounds remarkably familiar today.

Now that kind of demand for sensation is being met by television, and it's not just the tabloid shows. According to Dan Rather, "We are all to one degree or another going this—what I call—the gutless path. Fear rules every newsroom in America." If ratings go down, news directors are fired. "We've lost our backbone," says Rather. "We've lost our guts . . . we fold when the going gets tough . . . we follow the herd. If everybody says Bobbitt is a story, everybody leads with Bobbitt, everybody goes with Bobbitt."[3] Competition for ratings also influences the content of the programs. "They've got us putting more and more fuzz and wuzz [police and dead bodies] on the air," says Rather, "so as to compete not with other news programs but with entertainment programs, including those posing as news programs."[4]

Steve Rendall says that many people do not understand what television really sells. "They sell audiences to sponsors," he says. "They're in the business to get as many people watching as they can, and to turn them over to Proctor and Gamble for 30 seconds for $125,000. . . . The news show isn't really the product. . . . What their product is is an audience, and that's what they get paid for." Rendall calls the programming the pretty packaging and says "the tabloidism is a natural . . . when you're trying to display shiny things for people to look at."[5]

Who should determine what is news and what isn't? Speaking to fellow journalists at a conference held at Columbia

University, Allan Neuharth said that it is "not you or I, not the editor of *The New York Times,* not the president of network news, not the publisher of the *Columbia Journalism Review,* but the general public." Neuharth added that some of the same critics who called *USA Today* "McPaper" are now stealing all of its McNuggets.[6]

But not everyone agrees that audiences should get what they want. Andrew Lack, president of NBC News, quoted Dick Salant, former president of CBS News (now deceased) as saying "We in broadcast journalism cannot, should not, and will not base our judgments on what we think the viewers and listeners are most interested in. . . . Our job is to give people not what they want, but what we think they ought to have."[7]

Some say concern over ratings may serve as a censoring mechanism. Subjects not considered juicy enough are never dealt with, no matter how important they are and how many people they affect. Emotional stories attract viewers and raise ratings. High ratings mean big bucks.

Body-Bag Journalism—If it Bleeds, it Leads

People have always been fascinated by other peoples' tragedies. During the Civil War, newspapers' circulations went up dramatically due to their coverage of the bloodshed. Wilbur F. Storey of the *Chicago Times* told one Civil War correspondent: "Telegraph fully all news you can get and when there is no news send rumours."[8]

Reporters have continued to go to great lengths for a sensational story. In 1912, reporters dressed as doctors and priests to get by barricades to interview *Titanic* survivors when they arrived in New York. In 1928, Tom Howard, a photographer for the *New York Daily News*, arranged to be an official witness at the execution of Ruth Snyder, who had been convicted of murdering her husband. Howard strapped a camera to his ankle, and when the electric-chair switch was thrown, he snapped the picture. The moment-of-death photo was responsible for the sale of 250,000 extra copies that day. The *News* later printed and sold another 750,000.[9] During the World War II years, Robert St. John, an Associated Press correspondent, remarked that "we were just leeches, reporters trying to suck headlines out of all this death and suffering." Things were not much different on the home front. Newsreel camera crews would sometimes pour several gallons of water on the roadway near a car accident before filming. On black-and-white film, the water looked like blood.[10]

Critics say that local television news programs in particular seem to focus on sensationalism. In 1977, Ron Powers described the topics covered by local news programs in an article for the *Columbia Journalism Review:* "Unending reports on sex fantasies. And runaway wives. And UFOs. And celebrities. And fires. And murders. And accidents. And, oh yes, the weather and sports."[11] The reason? Ratings. Roone Arledge, president of ABC News and Sports, says, "most local stations live and die by the Nielsen ratings of their local news, which has become one of their biggest profit centers. I think it's a very dangerous trend."[12]

Richard Smith of *Newsweek* criticizes local news programs for providing segment after segment of "blood, bullets, and tears." He says local news shows are expanding their hours but still offering little or no analysis and making virtually no effort to address the serious issues in their communities. David Smith, a top executive with Frank Magid Associates, which advises stations on improving news ratings, puts it this way:

War has always drawn audiences. These images of American troops in Saudi Arabia were used to report on the Persian Gulf War.

"Murder, especially black-on-black murder, is a critically important story. But are you really telling that story one body bag at a time?"[13] Howard Kurtz says, "I see in a lot of these stories [local television news] not only an attempt to titillate and an attempt to grab viewers, but somehow it seems, perhaps subliminally, an attempt to frighten. And it is spreading like a computer virus."[14]

Violent crime figures have actually dropped in most areas, but you'd never know it by watching the local television news. During the week of May 8, 1994, the Los Angeles affiliate of FAIR monitored all thirty-five hours of local late-night news. They found that 23 to 54 percent of the coverage dealt with crime. There were lots of dramatic visuals of police tapes, surveillance footage, fires, and explosions. But nothing was said that might help people understand the causes of crime or possible solutions. At the same time, only two of the seven local stations mentioned an upcoming election. Of 2,059 minutes of news, just over 8 minutes concerned the election.[15]

George Gerbner, director of the Annenberg School of Communications at the University of Pennsylvania, has studied heavy television viewers. Those who watch four hours, or more, a day have what Gerbner calls the "mean world syndrome"—feelings of danger, mistrust, intolerance, gloom, and hopelessness. They grossly overestimate the incidence of crime and violence.[16] A study by the Annenberg's Survey Research Center showed that of people who are heavy television viewers, almost 24 percent say there is a "very serious" chance that they will be victimized, while only 16 percent of light television viewers feel that way. Among heavy viewers, 48 percent say it is not safe to walk on their streets at night, while only 29 percent of light viewers feel that way.

James Fyfe, professor of criminal justice at Temple University, says that people come to think they are in great danger because the media tend to show middle-class victims.[17] This can create a vicious cycle: people become fearful, buy guns, overreact to any perceived threat, and thus increase the chance for violence. The media also promote an "us vs. them" mentality by portraying law-abiding, white, middle-class victims as having to be constantly on guard against lower-class and minority criminals.

Glen Pierce, director of Northeastern University's Center of Applied Social Research, believes that by misrepresenting the crime problem, reporters are frightening people and driving

61

them to the political right. He says that is why voters are growing more conservative and punitive in their politics.[18]

One of the most notorious local news broadcasts is WSVN (Channel 7) in Miami, Florida. A typical one-hour newscast can include as many as fifty stories with titles like "Mauled to Death" or "Tiny Victims." An in-house composer creates dramatic music to accompany horrifying images. Anchorman Rick Sanchez has the ability, according to *Miami Herald* columnist Carl Hiaasen, to "make a routine domestic shooting sound like a sniper attack at an orphanage." One story aired by the station included a tape recording of a woman's desperate 911 call. She can be heard screaming, "Can you please send an officer here? My husband has a gun to me." Then a gunshot is heard and more screaming. Three more gunshots. Then the screaming stops, and the line goes dead.

Critics say the program seems to wallow in violence. When a Bengal tiger fatally mauled a zookeeper, WSVN covered the death seventeen times in a single day, complete with pictures of the bloody body. Channel 7 broadcasts eight hours of news a day and offers what they call "stories that chill the flesh and warm the heart."[19]

At the other end of the spectrum is WCCO-TV in Minneapolis, Minnesota. Responding to viewer complaints, the station edits its 5 P.M. newscast so that it is "family sensitive." They cover the same stories, but rather than focusing on bloodstains and body bags, a report might show the victim's home or a family photograph. Crime stories include information indicating whether the incident was unusual or part of a crime wave.

The idea of family-oriented news programs has spread to other areas of the country. While some say this is a step ahead, others worry that it is a form of censorship. "This is very dangerous," says Terry Heaton, news director of WRIC in Richmond, Virginia. "Censorship is just a stone's throw away, and this is an era when people are throwing stones. If we say we're part of the problem, what's to keep some governmental body from saying: 'Well, if you're part of the problem, you don't have to be here at all?'" Others feel that the idea has merit. Stephanie Brady of Children Now, a children's advocacy group, says that "if they [children] see people like themselves continually as chalk marks or in handcuffs, it makes them sad or angry. We need a higher degree of responsibility toward reflecting reality."[20]

Does Violent Television Create Violent People?

In 1960, Dr. Leonard D. Eron, a psychology professor at Yale University, conducted a study to find out what makes children aggressive. He suspected that it had to do with how the children were treated by their parents. Ten years later, he was surprised to find that the best predictor of aggression among the children (who were now teenagers) was not how their parents treated them, but how much television they watched. Another ten years later, he found again that those who watched more television (they were now adults) were more aggressive. Dr. Eron "found that the violent programming they had watched was related to the seriousness of the crimes they committed, how aggressive they were to their spouses, and even to how aggressive their own kids were."[21]

However, does television viewing cause the aggression or do aggressive children watch more television? The majority of people who have studied the relationship feel that there is a connection, but the exact nature of it is difficult to pin down. And some studies have shown no link at all.

63

Critics are concerned that children see too much violence on television.

Although watching violence on television may not cause violent acts, it may desensitize viewers to violence. That is, viewers may become used to violence and therefore not be shocked or repulsed by it. Researchers estimate that the average child will see 100,000 acts of simulated violence by the end of elementary school. However, it is an unfortunate reality that many children are exposed to violence in their own homes and neighborhoods, whether or not they see it on television.

People can never figure things out for themselves: they have to see them acted out by actors.

—Robert Frost[1]

6

Reality-based TV

Twirling his big, black mustache, the villain ties a beautiful girl to the railroad tracks. "Nya, ah ah," he cackles. The music builds. Then a spirited "I'll save you" is heard and the hero gallops up on his white horse. "Curses, foiled again," grumbles the villain. Old-time melodrama. Victims and villains. Simple. Predictable. People loved it.

Today's reality-based television is not much different. The programs look like drama, but they show events that actually happened, sometimes as they happen. They show the people who were actually involved, sometimes adding professional actors. And, like the old melodramas, they often boil down to the good guys against the bad.

Live and On the Scene

One of the most famous on-the-scene reports of all time was on May 6, 1937. Herbert Morrison, a staff announcer for

WLS in Chicago, was waiting for the *Hindenburg* airship (blimp) to arrive at Lakehurst, New Jersey. Morrison described the scene for a radio audience as the *Hindenburg*, filled with seven million cubic feet of highly-flammable hydrogen, unexpectedly burst into flames. Morrison's live report (which was preserved on audio discs) is chilling even today: "It's crashing! Oh, my! Get out of the way, please. And the folks——. Oh, it's terrible! This is one of the worst catastrophes in the world. . . . Oh, the humanity! All the passengers! All the people screaming around here. . . . I'm going to step inside where I can't see it. I tell you it's terrible. Folks, I must stop for a minute. I've lost my voice. It's the worst thing I've ever witnessed."[2]

Television news-camera crews usually aren't there to capture a story as it happens. But reality-based program crews travel with police and rescue personnel, filming actual drug busts, rescues, and accident scenes as they occur. Cameras move with the police, increasing the sense of immediacy. The in-your-face action is exciting and unpredictable.

Some say that the presence of cameras can change the way people behave and may even alter the outcome of the event. Proponents say filming arrests may reduce violence—by cops and suspects. But members of the Police Executive Research Forum say that the presence of television crews actually encourages police officers to behave more aggressively.[3] Suspects may also show increased bravado and be less likely to back down from confrontations—for fear of appearing wimpy on television.

What is reality? Whose reality?

Legendary CBS news anchor Walter Cronkite always signed off his evening news program with: "And that's the way it is."

He was showing more confidence in the relationship between reality and television reporting than perhaps we would show now. Today, reality shows use on-the-scene video cameras to record real events. But they also use reenactments. Even though they look like documentaries, reality-based television shows are as carefully photographed and edited as movies. Cinematic lighting, special effects, moody background music, and narration are added to enhance the drama. "Bad guys" are made to look more threatening. Film footage of real events is mixed with scenes that have been recreated.

Reality-based shows don't have to follow the rules of news production. As entertainment programming, they do not have to worry about accuracy, fairness, or balance. In real life, accused criminals seldom admit guilt, and the details of a crime may never be known. But through visuals like a sinister hand on a doorknob or a car driving down a dark road, events can be reenacted. Alan Wurtzel, an ABC senior vice president, says the "point of view" camera is a storytelling device that's justified provided it doesn't distort the truth.[4] Others say the technique conveys a seamlessness and certainty to story lines, which they feel is distorting.[5] The mixing of real and fictional (or at least reenacted) scenes can be confusing to viewers. A reenactment can be so realistic that viewers believe that the event really happened. PBS producer Hedrick Smith says that "television has a special impact and, therefore, a special responsibility. . . . Whether it's really true or not, people believe what they see. They trust their eyes."[6]

Reality programs are cheap to produce and get high ratings. The people involved in the events are usually happy to cooperate since they are shown in a positive light either as brave heroes or innocent victims. But they're not the only ones eager to help.

Cops as Heroes

Most police departments cooperate freely with the reality shows. "People used to think law enforcement was like *Dirty Harry* or 'Miami Vice,'" says Nick Navarro, sheriff in Broward County, Florida. "Shows like 'Cops' let the American people see what the police are really like."[7] More cynical observers say that police departments like the shows because they glamorize police officers.

Unlike documentaries, which show the good and the bad, reality-based shows generally show only the good. Police officers are always in the right. Emergency personnel never show poor judgment or make mistakes. This, say critics, is no accident.

Producers of reality-based programs rely on the cooperation of the public agencies involved. If their operations were shown in a bad light, the agencies would cut off access and there would be no program. So the shows edit out unflattering scenes and edit in dramatic ones. They often allow the agencies to have a say in what is shown. The result is that viewers often don't get the whole story.

Police Chief Jay Carey of Newport News, Virginia, says: "They don't doctor the tapes, but they only depict a portion of policing—the portion that satiates the public's appetite for violence."[8] "It is propaganda of the worst kind," says Joe Saltzman, a professor of journalism and associate mass media editor of *USA Today*, "because it looks so real, so true-to-life, while in reality it is wrong-headed and dangerous to a society's well-being."[9] Steve Rendall says "they're a fraud. There's nothing real about them." Rendall says the shows are a sort of social control—to show why we should obey authority:

> Never do you see any police brutality . . . never do you hear police utter racist words. I'm not saying that most

police are brutal or racist, I'm just saying that if it was reality-based, it would happen every now and then. It *does* happen. Police are like other human beings.[10]

Not all police departments support the reality-based programs. The Chicago police department does not allow camera crews in squad cars, and San Diego's police have refused cooperation with most of the reality-based police shows. But most seem to enjoy the positive publicity. Sheriff Navarro has become something of a celebrity from his appearances on "Cops" and has even been criticized on local media for taking too many trips to promote the show.[11]

A Question of Privacy

In 1992, a woman and her four-year-old son were in their Brooklyn apartment when Secret Service agents suddenly showed up to look for evidence that the woman's husband (who wasn't home) had committed credit-card fraud. One of the agents had invited a television crew from the now defunct CBS "Street Stories" show to come along on the raid. As the agents began searching the home, the television cameras rolled. The woman protested, covering her face and her son's with a magazine. Although the footage never aired, the woman sued for invasion of privacy. An appeals court ruled that the Secret Service had no right to allow the television crew, or even unauthorized law-enforcement personnel, to enter a private home. Although some journalists warned of the decision's "chilling effect" on news gathering, the three-judge panel said that "a private home is not a sound stage for law-enforcement theatricals."[12]

People have often said that journalists violate people's right to privacy by intruding on them in times of tragedy.

What is learned from interviews with grieving mothers who have lost children in apartment fires? Don't we already know the answer to the question "how do you feel?" The same holds for photographs and videotapes of what should be private moments. Carl E. Lindstrom, a former editor, suggests that "the picture which creates in the beholder the feeling of intrusion upon grief or private anguish, the feeling of 'here I should not be,' ought never to be taken."[13]

A Diet of Tragedy

As the speeding train hits the car, glass shatters, and the car spins around. There is crying, screaming, and panic. Even though it is a reenactment, it is hard to watch without squirming. Yet scenes like this one from "Rescue 911" captivate people.

When people watch hour after hour of gruesome accidents, near-drownings, shootings, house fires, and other tragedies from their comfortable living-room chairs, does it affect them? Are they being trained to sit and watch without taking any action to help people, or are they learning what to do in case of an emergency? Are we training people to be heroes, or just giving them a more sophisticated way to gawk at car accidents?

Tom Colbert, president of Industry R&D, a firm that searches out many of the stories later covered by the media, looks for situations from which something can be learned. He likes stories that have an underlying moral. At the very least, the story should have "some good twists and turns," says Colbert. However, he just suggests story ideas; he doesn't control which ones are picked up. And the selection of stories is often simply a matter of what the producers find appealing. Some very real stories may be ignored because they are too depressing, the people involved are not attractive enough, or the subject matter is too controversial for sponsors.

Tragic stories may also feed a hunger for folklore and morality plays. The O.J. Simpson story, with its fallen hero, takes on the proportions of a Greek tragedy. The incident in which Tonya Harding allegedly arranged to have Nancy Kerrigan injured so that she could not compete exposed a naked rivalry that people found fascinating.[14] Deborah Prothrow-Stith, M.D., former commissioner of Public Health for the State of Massachusetts and now an assistant dean at the Harvard School of Public Health, compares today's television dramas that depict lurid crimes committed against women and children to the cowboy stories of early television. She points out that, as in the cowboy melodramas, editing and music seduce the viewer and make horrifying events appear dramatic and thrilling.[15]

Literary agent Bill Birnes says that "what happens on the news takes a lot of mental work to put together."[16] Reality-based shows pre-digest stories and provide an easily understood narrative. A complicated world is boiled down into the good guys (us), and the bad guys (them). Unfortunately, this idea feeds the "mean world syndrome." People who routinely watch these shows (perhaps in addition to viewing crime-ridden local news broadcasts) may get the idea that they are surrounded by individuals who want to rob, rape, or murder them, and that being victimized is inevitable.

Catching Bad Guys

An employment placement worker in Charlotte, North Carolina, was watching television when she saw a preview for "America's Most Wanted." The show was to feature the

71

John Walsh is host of "America's Most Wanted," a show that uses viewer tips to capture suspects.

story of a man who was suspected of killing his estranged wife and fleeing with their sons. The Charlotte woman was about to turn off the television when she realized that the man shown on the preview had come to her office earlier in the week looking for a job. The woman called police, giving them the telephone number the man had left. Police traced the number, alerted the FBI, and together they captured the suspect.

According to the producers, "America's Most Wanted" has helped in the capture of almost three hundred fifty fugitives. The series features reenactments of crimes based on police records, witness accounts, and court testimony. Viewers with tips are asked to call the show's toll-free hotline. Karen Daborowski, the show's production associate, says that when calls come in, "a lot of people get involved. They don't just do it because it's a job. They do it because they really care about catching the criminals."[17] The show also has a weekly feature on missing children and produces "The Missing Child Alert" public service announcements, which are distributed to all television outlets. Between November 1992 and January 1995, eight of the featured children were recovered. The series host, John Walsh, is an advocate for missing and exploited children. His son, Adam, was abducted and murdered in 1981.

At least twelve new reality-based shows were marketed at an industry conference in 1995. The shows included series about the Coast Guard, border patrols, con artists, and emergency room teams, as well as more police shows. "To the viewers, real life is stranger than fiction," says Chuck Larson, president of MTM Distribution, which syndicates "Rescue 911." "There is nothing as gripping as watching a rescue—each story has heros [sic]."[18] Larson says that "nightly news is depressing. 'Rescue 911' is an uplifting and positive show that leaves people feeling good." Sid Cohen, president of "LAPD" distributor MGM Domestic Television, adds that "police dramas have been around for forty years and they will always be around; this is just another form of that drama."[19]

Proponents of reality-based television say that it provides positive role models for children and shows them that police officers and emergency personnel can help them. The shows may also teach people what to do in an emergency. For example, children have learned how to dial "911" from watching "Rescue 911."

Critics charge that such shows are blurring the line between fact and fiction. They are concerned that viewers may confuse real life (fact), reality-based programs (fact combined with some fiction), and shows such as "Baywatch" that are purely fiction.

How many times do I have to kill before I get a name in the paper or some national attention?

—A serial killer in Kansas, in a letter to police.[1]

7

Ethics in Journalism

Some people would say that the words "journalism and ethics" belong together as much as, say "used-car dealers and honesty." Nonetheless, most journalists follow a strict code of professional standards. Two of the most important standards are ethical as well as professional: accuracy and fairness.[2]

Some say that journalistic ethics are slipping. Formerly sacred rules such as those against paying sources and secretly taping people have become, to paraphrase Bill Murray in *Ghostbusters*, "more of a guideline really." Is this good for the public? Are we learning more or losing more?

Peeping Tom Journalism

Reporters constantly struggle with what and how much to tell. Sometimes the facts are clear. Other times, journalists must rely on their own judgment.

A retired minister in a small town does not return from a
fishing trip. Police find his car parked about halfway to the
lake. It is locked and undamaged. In it they find a half-eaten
ham sandwich, fishing tackle, a gun with one shell fired, and a
copy of *Penthouse* (a magazine that contains pictures of naked
women). The minister is missing. You're the reporter and
your story is due. What do you report? Suppose the minister
just went for a walk? Do you risk his embarrassment and
mention the magazine? Is the gun important? Should you
propose any theories about what might have happened?

The reporter who actually faced these decisions decided to
mention the gun, the sandwich, the fishing tackle, and the
condition of the car, but not the magazine or any speculation.
The minister's body was later found. He had been killed by a
hitchhiker, who had left the magazine in the minister's car.[3]

In the old days, reporters knew politicians (including
Presidents) who slept around, movie stars who were gay, and
public figures who used drugs or abused alcohol. They just
kept it to themselves. Now, at least in part because the public
seems to have an endless hunger for it, reporters sometimes
cover these aspects of celebrities' lives more than any other.

Some of the interest can be justified on the basis that
character affects how people perform their jobs. But what if
the information isn't relevant? For example, does the public
need to know that a senator is gay? When a famous person
dies, does the public have a right to all the details? Should the
public know which public figures are unfaithful to their
spouses? Are these things we *need* to know or just things we
want to know?

When Gennifer Flowers alleged a twelve-year affair with
President Bill Clinton, she first sold the story to the tabloid
Star. CNN reported the story and so did the networks and the

major newspapers and newsmagazines. Peter Jennings, anchor for ABC's "World News Tonight," was against broadcasting the Flowers story without further reporting by ABC correspondents, but says, "it was made clear to [me] . . . that if you didn't go with the story, every [ABC] affiliate in the country would look up and say, 'What the hell's going on in this place? Don't they know a story when they see it?'"[4]

Some stories receive such wide visibility that to ignore them is to "play ostrich man," says Shelby Coffey, editor of *The Los Angeles Times*. "You have to give your readers some perspective on the information they're getting."[5]

Scrutiny may be the price one pays for fame. But what about relatives of celebrities? Are they fair game too? And what about the average person?

When Sara Jane Moore pointed a gun at President Gerald Ford, a man in the crowd knocked her hand, deflecting the shot. The man, Oliver W. Sipple, became an instant hero. He was thirty-three years old and a marine veteran. What else did the public want or need to know about him? Initial reports did not mention Sipple's sexual orientation. But when a *San Francisco Chronicle* columnist said that local gay leaders were proud of Sipple's actions, other papers began to report it. Sipple sued the columnist and several newspapers for invading his privacy. He said he had suffered "great mental anguish, embarrassment and humiliation." Lawyers argued that by becoming involved in an event of worldwide importance, Sipple had given up part of his right to privacy, because the public has a legitimate interest in his activities.[6]

Rosa Lopez was a maid, working quietly and anonymously until she became a key witness in the O.J. Simpson trial. Suddenly, she was the focus of intense scrutiny. Lopez was hounded by cameras and reporters everywhere she went.

Her every move was analyzed. She eventually returned to her native country to escape the pressure, only to find that the media followed her there. How many witnesses will come forward in the future, knowing what kind of treatment awaits them? Do people who accidently find themselves involved in such high-profile cases have rights, or do we deserve to know everything about them?

Reporting News or Making News?

Sometimes reporters or camera crews have been accused of interfering with, rather than just recording events. Other times they have been criticized for not interfering when they should have.

One night, in Anniston, Alabama, WHMA-TV received several calls from a man who seemed drunk. The caller asked station employees whether anyone would like to see "somebody set himself on fire" in the town square in Jacksonville. The camera crew on duty thought that the man was joking, but called the police anyway. Officers searched the square but found nothing and left. The camera crew set up their equipment anyway. Before long, the caller appeared and, as cameras rolled, tried twice to ignite his clothes, which had been drenched with lighter fluid. Then, as the cameras continued to roll, he poured more fluid on himself and tried a third match. This time, the clothes caught fire. As he sat on the ground in front of the camera, the flames started to spread. Then the fire erupted, engulfing his body. As the man stood to run, the camera operator shouted to his colleague to put out the fire. He tried, but couldn't. The camera then followed the burning man as he ran across the square. A volunteer fire fighter saw what was happening and put out the fire with an extinguisher.

Would the man have set himself on fire if the cameras had not been there? What was the television crew's responsibility? The camera operator involved was quoted as saying "My job is to record events as they happen."[7] But should he have tried harder to prevent this event?

The media often play a role in events, whether they mean to or not. Would terrorists set bombs, hijack planes, or take hostages if the media never mentioned a word about it? If there was no publicity for their cause, no visibility for their actions, and no showcase for their demands, would they bother?

Another concern is whether television cameras should be allowed in courtrooms. Having cameras in the courtroom educates the public. It's entertaining. It also can affect the outcome of the trial.

Susanne Roschwalb, associate professor of public communication at The American University in Washington, D.C. and co-editor of *Litigation Public Relations*, says that "the inclusion of the camera in the courtroom is having the biggest impact in bringing high-profile cases to the court of public opinion." Defendants can hire public relations specialists to make them look better. The prosecution and defense can, through the media, present their interpretation of the case, skewing the facts to their own advantage. Roschwalb says that "the camera can have a life-or-death effect on courtroom decisions." Prior to the O.J. Simpson trial, attorneys mentioned evidence that was later shown not to exist, and made unfounded suggestions designed to influence the viewing audience (which may have contained potential jurors). Is such use of the media appropriate?

79

On this issue, there is a conflict between the First Amendment, which protects the public's right to know, and the Sixth Amendment, which protects the defendant's right to a fair trial. According to Roschwalb, what is needed is for the lawyers, public relations experts, and media personnel to work together to produce coverage that is within agreed-upon ethical guidelines.[8]

Hidden Cameras and Other Tactics

On September 22, 1992, at a health club in Massapequa, New York, Amy Fisher (who had shot and permanently injured her lover's wife) laughed and talked with boyfriend Paul Makely about sex in jail and all she hoped to gain from her fame. Little did she know that "Hard Copy" had paid between $6,000 and $10,000 to Makely to carry a hidden video camera. The show aired the tape, which damaged Fisher's credibility in the case against Joey Buttafuoco for statutory rape.[9]

In November 1994, CBS's "60 Minutes" used hidden tape recorders and cameras while interviewing a freelance writer who didn't want to speak on the air. After it came to light, host Mike Wallace apologized to the writer and on the air. The president of CBS News issued a statement that said "It was a violation of journalistic ethics. . . . Without any question it was wrong."[10]

"60 Minutes" has long been known for the ambush interview. They catch the subject off-guard and hope that, unprepared, he or she will blurt out damaging information. While this may seem unfair if you are the person suddenly facing Mike Wallace, a rolling camera, and a microphone stuck in your face, audiences love to see scam artists and other bad guys on the hot seat. Some suggest that this approach be used only as a last resort after more conventional news gathering approaches have failed. Even Mike Wallace acknowledges that the ambush interview is dramatic but seldom provides much insight. He says, "If you're after light rather than heat, there's not much point in it."[11]

Even when the cameras are out in the open, questions of journalistic ethics can arise. Connie Chung, host of CBS' "Eye to Eye with Connie Chung," took a great deal of heat over an interview she did with Kathleen Gingrich, mother of Newt Gingrich, Speaker of the U.S. House of Representatives. After Mrs. Gingrich said during the interview that she couldn't tell Chung what her son had said about first lady Hillary Clinton, Chung suggested "why don't you just whisper it to me, just between you and me?" Mrs. Gingrich, whispered back "she's a bitch." The next day's newspapers trumpeted, "Newt Gingrich has called Hillary Clinton a 'bitch,' Gingrich's mother told CBS News in an interview."

Newt Gingrich called Chung's approach a "professionally disreputable act." *Newsweek* media analyst Jonathan Alter argued that saying it was just between the two of them was the equivalent of saying it was off the record. "They [CBS] had a choice," said Alter during an interview on "Inside Edition," "the pretty clear journalism ethics on one side or get a lot of attention for a show in a very competitive newsmagazine situation on the other and they went for the attention and the ratings."[12]

Colman McCarthy, *The Washington Post* columnist and founder of the Center for Teaching Peace, said that "'Between you and me' ought to mean exactly that—not 'between you, me and the public.'" He went a step further to ask what is the relevance of a "fluff interview" with the sixty-eight-year-old mother of the Speaker of the House. "Why not," asked

81

McCarthy, "a CBS News special on some elderly, sick and impoverished women in an urban tenement whose suffering will likely increase if the social welfare policies of Gingrich become law." McCarthy stated that even without the deceit he felt was involved in getting the remark, the bitch quote was "low-level gossip." He said that there are a range of legitimate methods for drawing out people, without resorting to trickery or lies.[13]

Did Connie Chung deceive Mrs. Gingrich? As Chung noted in her response to critics, "Mrs. Gingrich was sitting before three cameras and television lights, with a microphone on. It was clear that what she said would be broadcast." In addition, earlier in the interview Chung had suggested that the Speaker, having spent his youth in the North, was "kind of a yankee." Gingrich whispered, "I think so." Chung whispered back, "But we won't tell anybody." Gingrich then whispered, "OK." The "we won't tell anybody" (knowing that millions are watching) is a somewhat common joke on talk shows. Given that earlier exchange, did Mrs. Gingrich understand the comment "just between you and me" as a promise or as a joke?

In November 1992, Mike Wallace told *The Washington Post* that "You don't like to baldly lie but I have" in discussing the demands of getting a knockout story. Many stories would never come to light without some coercion, arm-bending, or even deception. Don Hewitt, executive producer of "60 Minutes," says, "It's the small crime versus the greater good."[14] The lines limiting how far journalists can go to get a terrific story continue to be tested.

Crime in Black and White

It was a compelling story. A young mother told police that someone had jumped into her car in a rural area of South

Carolina and then driven off with her two young sons. Two beautiful children snatched in broad daylight, by a stranger— a black stranger—with a gun. The small southern town rose up in outrage. Dozens of local, state, and federal investigators flocked to the area. But that was nothing compared to the swarm of reporters who, like yellow-jackets feeding on spilled soda, crawled over one another to lap up the details.

In all, some two hundred reporters covered the story from the scene. For nine days, law enforcement personnel and volunteers scoured the country for leads. The case was featured on "America's Most Wanted" and "A Current Affair." News conferences were broadcast live by CNN and local TV stations. The parents appeared on "Today" and "Good Morning America." The idea of a menacing black perpetrator preying on innocent white victims reinforced the fears of many whites.

Then the sad truth came out. The children were dead. Murdered not by the African-American man in the ski cap pictured in a composite sketch that was widely distributed, but by a much more likely suspect—their own mother.

What was so appealing about this case that it created such a frenzy of interest? During the same period, other children disappeared, were beaten to death, died in car accidents, or drowned. Some suggest that the news media in general, and the tabloid shows in particular, favor stories that deal with appealing, usually white, victims and unknown, often black, villains. In a syndicated column, Claude Lewis said that the South Carolina case "fit neatly into our quiet belief that assailants are usually young, black and violent."[15]

The idea of an evil stranger abducting innocent, defenseless children is exciting and scary, but it is an image largely created by the media and people's imaginations. Far more children are kidnapped, hurt, or killed by their own parents or other

83

family members than by strangers. Each year about thirteen hundred children are murdered by their parents or close relatives. Of the nearly forty thousand kids reported missing between 1984 and 1994, only 4 percent where taken by strangers.[16]

In 1989, Charles Stuart claimed that an African-American man had forced his way into his car and shot him and his wife, Carol, during a robbery. Carol was shot in the head and died. For weeks, media coverage was intense. Who was this fiend who would kill a pregnant woman on her way home from childbirth class? In Boston, where the incident occurred, African-American men were stopped and questioned by police. An innocent man was arrested. As it turned out, Carol Stuart was killed, as most white female murder victims are, by her own husband.

In reality, poor minority citizens are the most frequent victims of crime. Yet these are not the stories television programs tend to feature. "No one wants to face how ordinary most assaults and most homicides are," says Deborah Prothrow-Stith. "No one wants to admit that the mass of these crimes involves plain people; acquaintances, family members, who drink, who disagree, who have a gun."[17]

Are television programs portraying a world divided into cops and criminals? Do they show a misleading number of African-American or Hispanic criminals and white victims? Have they created such a climate of fear and distrust that criminals can use that fear to deflect suspicion from themselves? "It's been clear in the black community for years that crimes have been committed by whites and blamed on blacks," says Carl Bell, president of the Community Mental Health Council of Chicago.[18]

A leading Hispanic civil rights organization, the National

Council of La Raza, says that reality-based shows are one of the worst offenders. Hispanics are either not portrayed at all or are portrayed as criminals, according to La Raza. The organization says that Hispanics are more likely than any other ethnic group to be portrayed committing crimes.[19]

A *USA Today*/CNN/Gallup Poll on news coverage of minority issues found that 62 percent of African-American respondents found themselves angered at least once a week about how the media deal with race/ethnicity-specific coverage; 55 percent of African Americans and 34 percent of Hispanics surveyed felt that the national television news media treat members of their racial or ethnic group unfairly in crime coverage. Among those who say coverage is unfair, at least three fourths say serious harm is done to members of their racial or ethnic group by the coverage.[20] Walter Jacobson, former news anchor at Chicago's WBBM, says that "children of the inner city are learning about themselves through the local news, and all they see is one black man after another dragged from a paddy wagon to a police station."[21]

African Americans and Hispanics aren't the only ones complaining about the media coverage they get. Young people complain that they are always shown as troublemakers. Teenage prostitutes, runaways, drug addicts, and juvenile offenders can get on talk shows, but a teenager who is getting good grades and saving money for college usually cannot.

Krista Bradford, who spent five years in the tabloid TV business, notes that tabloids run few stories on African Americans (except as perpetrators or criminals), gays, or unattractive women. When she proposed stories for "A Current Affair," she recalls being asked what color the person was and being asked for pictures. Stories dealing with these "unwanted people" generally were not pursued, according to

Bradford, although she says this may have improved since her time there.[22]

Responsibility vs. Censorship

It was a routine news conference in Harrisburg, Pennsylvania, on January 22, 1987. The state treasurer, R. Budd Dwyer, had just finished reading a statement in which he accused the media of hounding him about alleged misdeeds. Then he told the television news crews, "you don't want to take down your equipment yet." Reaching into a manila envelope, he pulled out a .357 magnum handgun. As cameras rolled and horrified reporters watched in disbelief, he waved the gun around, put the barrel in his mouth, and pulled the trigger. It was 11 A.M. Every news organization, local and national, had access to a videotape of the suicide. What, if anything, would they show on the noon news shows?

TV news directors were forced to make a quick and difficult decision. In Philadelphia, WPVI (Channel 6) was the only station that aired the entire videotape of the suicide on the noon newscast. WCAU (Channel 10) faded to black after showing Dwyer with the gun in his mouth, and KYW (Channel 3) cut the tape even sooner. By early-evening newscasts, Channels 6 and 10 had edited footage to a point comparable to Channel 3's and aired warnings before showing the tape. Lancaster NBC affiliate WGAL cut the video but allowed the audio to run. "You heard the crack of the gun," news director Ed Wickenheiser said, "But you didn't see the back of his head being blown off." On national newscasts, NBC and CNN showed footage of Dwyer waving the gun; CBS and ABC reported the story without showing any video.

While some defended the airing of the complete tape,

feeling that it was appropriate and not exploitative, others disagreed. Philadelphia's Channel 3 news director Randy Covington, who heard the initial reports on the radio, immediately called the station and ordered that the tape be edited.

> I don't think it's journalism. . . . It's irresponsible. There were people in this newsroom who saw the whole tape and were shocked, appalled, sick to their stomach. Some were crying. That's not something that needed to be shown, in my opinion. I felt we could tell the story better by not showing the whole tape than by simply putting on a gruesome and tragic act that, in my opinion, serves no purpose and is disrespectful to the family of the deceased.[23]

During the Vietnam War, a man suspected of being a Viet Cong was brought to the head of the South Vietnam police, Brigadier General Nguyen Ngoc Loan, for questioning. NBC-TV reporters were there with cameras rolling when the general put a gun to the man's head and pulled the trigger. Film footage showed not only the shooting but the victim lying on the ground with blood spurting out of his head. NBC executive producer Robert Northshield had to decide whether to use the graphic footage.

The decision involved not only ethics and taste, but journalistic responsibility. It was a news event that Americans had a right to know about. Northshield decided to run the film only to the point at which the man hit the ground, and then go to black for three seconds. Some people felt that the film shouldn't have been shown at all, yet others thought the entire film should have been aired. One staff member later said that Americans were getting a "too sanitized" picture of the war, and they should have "their noses rubbed in" the violence and gore. The still photo of the execution won a Pulitzer

Prize for Associated Press photographer Eddie Adams and appeared on page one of both *The New York Times* and *The Washington Post.* It's one of the most famous news photographs and certainly one of the most remembered.[24]

Many people feel that the vivid pictures of the Vietnam War contributed to the United States withdrawal. Never before had Americans seen the reality of war right in their living rooms. The war was no longer just a cocktail conversation or even a newspaper article; it was the bloodied bodies people could see for themselves on the television screen.

Arguments continue about just how much raw truth should be shown on television. On one side are the people who argue that not reporting violence misleads the public, gives them a false sense of security, and takes away the outrage that pushes people to take action to change things. On the other side are people concerned that violence harms children, desensitizes us to human suffering, and is trivialized by being presented in between sitcoms and quiz shows.

Accuracy vs. Fact Manipulation

When "Dateline NBC" reported on alleged fire hazards in older General Motors (GM) pickups, it simulated the type of impact that was suspected of causing the fuel tank to rupture. Sure enough, the truck caught fire. Later, it was found that the test truck had been fitted with toy rocket engines to make sure spilled gasoline would catch fire. On a subsequent show, anchors Jane Pauley and Stone Phillips read a retraction. It included a list of flaws in the test, the most significant being that a fuel tank NBC said had ruptured upon impact had actually remained intact.

If news media use "don't let the facts get in the way of a

good story" as a guideline, they become like the boy who cried wolf. When it comes time to expose a really dangerous situation, no one will believe them. This sort of thing is also happening in print media. But what makes television different, says Penn State professor Steven Knowlton, co-editor of the book *The Journalist's Moral Compass,* is its pressing need for visual drama, which can push producers to embellish the facts. The result is a loss of credibility. "Dateline NBC" didn't need to rig the truck, he says, but did to make sure it would work. They ended up having to apologize. GM came off looking like wounded good guys.[25]

The media have also been accused of exaggerating dangers to scare the public. When a Florida man filed suit alleging that a cellular phone had caused his wife's fatal brain tumor, the media played up the possible risks. Often as scientifically illiterate as the general public, reporters misuse statistics, mis-understand the scientific process, and mistake caution for alarm. "The media are in the outrage business," says Peter Sandman, a consultant who helps companies talk about risk.[26] Getting out of a moving car is risky. So is getting out of bed. Sandman says journalists often don't help people sort out the degrees of risk.

Richard Smith says that "the nasty little secret of televi-sion news, and to some increasing degree the print press today, is its bias. I'm not talking about the kind of bias that people on the far left or far right accuse us in the media of, but a bias towards controversy, towards heat, towards emo-tion." Smith says that if you take any issue, "the forty-five seconds that you will get on most television newscasts will include hot and powerful sound bites that invariably reflect the outer extremes of the debate."[27] Smith says this practice reinforces the impression of society as highly polarized and squeezes out the middle ground.

Some people feel that the bias goes much deeper. Steve Rendall says "the product has been filtered through sort of a corporate-friendly sift." In addition, says Rendall, political opinion is restricted. "To paraphrase Dorothy Parker, the media consumer in America is getting the spectrum from A to B. They're getting very narrow viewpoints."[28]

Show Business vs. Science

A "Leeza" show devoted to miracles featured a religious painting that cried, people who bleed from the hands (like Christ on the cross), and a man who claimed to have been miraculously cured of a fatal disease. The audience seemed to believe that the only explanation for these phenomena is that they are miracles. But there were no alternative theories presented. This left viewers with the impression that none exist, when of course they do. Such biased reporting is becoming increasingly common.

Healthy skepticism—questioning the reports, demanding documentation, looking for other explanations—is often treated in a mocking way, if considered at all, on some of these shows. The hosts often accept guests' claims with little or no critical examination. Leeza ended the show on miracles with the advice, "So believe in miracles—they'll happen."

Contrast this with a "Donahue" show on the same subject. After discussing some of these phenomena, Donahue introduced Shawn Carlson, Ph.D., a physicist, astrophysicist, nuclear physicist, and part-time magician, who was able to make a picture of the Mona Lisa cry. The scientist proved that it is possible to make paintings and statues cry, for days or weeks unattended, through completely explainable means. And the tears have all the characteristics of human tears, including the saltiness—no miracles required.

Donahue did not say that miracles don't happen, and he was respectful to the people making the claims (including a woman who claimed to have seen the image of Jesus in a tortilla). However, he presented a much more balanced treatment of the same subject matter and allowed members of the audience to decide for themselves whether miracles happen.

If it gets in the way of a good show, accuracy can suffer, particularly on programs devoted to the exploration of supernatural activity. Experts appearing on these shows may be nothing more than parapsychologists or authors of books on the paranormal—people whose businesses rely on people believing such phenomena exist.

Studies show that the media unduly influence people to accept paranormal claims by giving excessive attention to the reports and by encouraging uncritical acceptance of them. Some have charged that the media behave totally irresponsibly in treating paranormal occurrences. They say that the principle of "seeing is believing" may be increasingly inadequate.[29]

If audiences had the ability to watch television critically—to reject what appeared false, to question the credibility of the "experts," to demand documentation—it would not matter as much. But most Americans are embarrassingly ignorant. And their gullibility assures that almost any viewpoint, no matter how extreme, will find converts.

8

What Does the Future Hold?

According to research studies, television news audiences are most interested in flames, blood, and sex, and least interested in ethnic news and labor news.[1] What do these interests say about us? Should news organizations be guided by what we want to know, what we need to know, or what we should know? Will children reared on entertainment news and scandal be prepared to compete in the world of the future? As we become more and more dependent upon television, these questions become even more important.

Influence on Viewers

First there were the Yuppies—Young, Upwardly-mobile Professional People. Now, according to Tom Colbert, we have the Guppes—kids that are Growing Up Practically

Parented by Electronics. These are the kids, Colbert says, with the three-minute attention spans.[2]

Some people question what the exposure to the mishmash of news and entertainment reporting is doing to today's teenagers. Some images are so real they may have cost the television crew their lives; others are carefully rigged up using actors, special effects, and fancy editing. Young people see a disconnected series of events from the openings of new stores to mass murders, without any historical, psychological, cultural, or ethical context.[3] And as attention spans get shorter, television provides less and less of the background information and analysis that is necessary to help audiences understand and interpret world events.

One of the most frequent complaints is that there is no *good* news. We hear about stranglings, car accidents, and drug overdoses, but never hear about good things. Andrew Lack, president of NBC News, says that "we too often now choose, without a moment's hesitation, the story that makes you feel usually repulsion, over the story that makes you think, which in television terms usually means boring."[4]

The increasing focus on human interest stories has, to some extent, actually increased the amount of good news we receive. People who overcame great odds, citizens fighting the system, miraculous recoveries, and similar success stories have become a common part of many news and information programs. These heart-warming stories reassure people that life isn't so bad.

Declining Standards?

Even though today's journalists are better equipped, have access to more information, and have better technology than ever before, very few Americans are informed enough to understand the events that affect them. Two thirds depend mainly on television for information, yet television is a superficial medium. Many news executives believe that Americans don't care about world news. They feel that people only care about the issues that have an obvious impact on themselves.

Many people feel that the high point of investigative reporting came when Bob Woodward and Carl Bernstein of *The Washington Post* uncovered the truth behind the Watergate break-in and cover-up, eventually forcing the resignation of President Richard Nixon. What broke the case was traditional, solid news reporting: tireless research, common sense, and hard work. It wasn't sexy. It wasn't gory. It was *journalism.*

Today, Carl Bernstein feels that the news business concentrates on not being behind or missing a major story "so speed and quantity substitute for thoroughness and quality, for accuracy and context." The pressure to compete, he says, creates a frenzied climate in which a "blizzard of information is presented and serious questions may not be raised."[5] Bernstein worries about the tabloidization of the news:

> For more than fifteen years, we have been moving away from real journalism toward the creation of a sleazoid info-tainment culture in which the lines between Oprah and Phil and Geraldo and Diane and even Ted . . . are too often indistinguishable. In this new culture of journalistic titillation, we teach our readers and our viewers that the trivial is significant, that the lurid and the loopy are more important than real news. We do not serve our readers and viewers, we pander to them. And we condescend to them, giving them what we think they want and what we calculate will sell and boost ratings and readership.[6]

Bernstein says that we are creating an "idiot culture." "What is happening today," he says, "unfortunately, is that the lowest form of popular culture—lack of information, misinformation, disinformation, and a contempt for the truth or the reality of most people's lives—has overrun real journalism." Bernstein says that, as a result of this concentration on unimportant issues, the press has missed most of the great stories of our generation from Iran-contra to the savings and loan scandal. He says that the press has not lived up to its responsibilities and that our current "talk show nation" is the result.[7]

A Look Toward the Future

Edward R. Murrow called television the greatest classroom in the world. But what is it teaching? We learn more about the lives of O.J. Simpson and Susan Smith than we do about health care or the environment. Will the full capability of television as an educational tool ever be realized, or will we allow it to be "chewing gum for the eyes," as architect and visionary Frank Lloyd Wright called it?

The way in which the news is gathered and reported will undoubtedly continue to evolve. Some foresee the development of the "video-journalist"—a reporter who carries a camera, shoots the story, and also reports it.[8]

Other trends that will likely continue are citizen involvement and interactive television. Local news organizations have picked up on the success of shows such as "America's Most Wanted" and "Unsolved Mysteries" that ask for tips on unsolved crimes or missing persons. Programs such as "Streetbeat" in Oxnard, California, broadcast information about neighborhood crime trends, seek help with unsolved

Shows like "Police Beat Live" in Charlotte, North Carolina, allow viewers to become involved in fighting crime.

crimes, and tell viewers how to prevent crime. A program called "Police Beat," airing in Charlotte, North Carolina, focuses on individual neighborhoods and shows what residents are doing to fight crime. Viewers can call in and speak directly to the police chief.

Cable networks are responding to audience demand by creating new products: The Talk Channel, E! Entertainment Television, and The Crime Channel (which features on-the-spot crime news and original productions as well as documentaries, movies, and series programs twenty-four hours a day).

The increasing sophistication of home computer and

telephone technology will draw the broadcasters and the audiences even closer together. And as we enter the information superhighway, James Willwerth says we'll have "yet another several hundred different ways" to expose and exploit celebrity and tragedy.[9]

Eventually, audiences may tire of the titillation. The market may already be flattening out, although the O.J. story certainly gave all news and entertainment media a boost. Circulation figures for print tabloids were down in 1993 from 1990. Ratings for "A Current Affair" dropped from 8.1 (1991 to 1992) to 6.6 (1993 to 1994), although "Hard Copy" went from 5.8 to 6.8 and "Inside Edition" rose from 6.5 to 7.3 (the percentage of all TV viewers who tune in on an average day).[10]

National Enquirer president Iain Calder says that audiences have not lost their appetite for scandal. "Look at the kind of people who are watching O.J. Simpson. Look at the network anchors spending so much time on this. It was inconceivable a number of years ago. The audience is much larger. It's almost everyone."[11]

Should journalists take a more active role in limiting sensationalism? Hedrick Smith thinks that journalists should at least think about what they are doing.

> I'm not saying we should ignore or stop our coverage of crime or conflict or corruption or social tensions and social problems . . . but I am asking whether or not we are telling the whole story to the audience. Do we have a vested interest in acting as the journalistic undertakers of our society, cashing in on society's calamities? Are we, in our concept of what is news, so committed to reporting the dramatic, the visual, the failures, the bad news, that we disregard good news as no news, and in that way, contribute, not only to declining standards in journalism, but declining values in our society as a whole?[12]

97

Steve Rendall says "there's got to be more public media in this country." He also suggests that young people who are really interested in becoming well informed should read, listen to, and watch the mainstream media but should also dig for alternative media.[13]

But what about the future of journalism in general? John Steinbeck, one of our greatest novelists and a former journalist, said in letter written in the 1930s:

> What can I say about journalism? It has the greatest virtue and the greatest evil. It is the first thing the dictator controls. It is the mother of literature and the perpetrator of crap. In many cases it is the only history we have. And yet it is the tool of the worst. But over a long period of time and because it is the product of so many, it is perhaps the purest thing we have. Honesty has a way of creeping in even when it was not intended.[14]

How to Be a Critical Viewer

1. BE SELECTIVE. Consciously choose programs, don't just leave the television on. Question whether your time could be better spent doing something else (it usually can be).

2. CONSIDER THE SOURCE. Remember that commercial television exists to make money and that the money comes from corporations (advertisers). Corporations, not viewers, are television's customers. Television is big business and that affects what is presented and how it is presented.

3. READ. Get a more thorough understanding of current issues by reading newspapers, books, and magazines, including alternative media. Look for context, not just for "sound bites."

4. DON'T BELIEVE EVERYTHING YOU SEE. Do your own research to confirm or dispute what you see on television. Remember that the media focus on things that are

out of the ordinary. What they portray does not represent the "normal," only the "interesting."

5. EXAMINE. Remember that technology can create "realities" that do not exist. If it seems too good (or bad) to be true, it probably is. Learn to recognize camera tricks, special effects, and other techniques that can alter the information being presented.

6. BE SKEPTICAL. Ask yourself whether what is being presented makes sense, is backed up by credible documentation, and is being communicated by someone who is an authority.

7. CONSIDER BIAS. Realize that even the most professional and respected news journalists bring their own feelings, prejudices, experiences, allegiances, and attitudes to their jobs.

8. QUESTION. Consider the motivations of the people involved. Are they looking to make money? Do they have hidden agendas? What they are getting out of being on television may affect what they say and do.

9. BE AN ACTIVE VIEWER. Write letters to program producers expressing your reactions to their programs (their addresses appear in most telvision listing guides). Talk with others about what you have seen. Listen to other interpretations. Look for alternative explanations. Decide for yourself what is important.

10. THINK. Use common sense. Don't assume that something that gets a lot of press coverage is important, and don't dismiss something just because it has not gotten a lot of attention. Use your own judgment.

Chapter Notes

Chapter 1

1. Orson Welles, *New York Herald Tribune* (October 12, 1956).

2. Penelope Patsuris, "O.J. By the Numbers," *TV Guide* (July 30, 1994), p. 19.

3. Ibid.

4. Larry Reibstein with Mark Miller, Charles Fleming, and Patrick Rogers, "Live From Nielsen Heaven," *Newsweek* (January 30, 1995), p. 49.

5. Trip Gabriel, "More and More of Us Have had our Fill of O.J.," *The Charlotte Observer* (November 28, 1994), pp. 1E–2E.

6. Barbara Johnson, "O.J. Simpson and Domestic Abuse: Where Were the Media Then?," *EXTRA!* (September/October, 1994), pp. 13–14.

7. Jeff Cohen and Norman Solomon, "We Interrupt Your O.J. Simpson Coverage . . .," *EXTRA!* (September/October, 1994), pp. 12–13.

Chapter 2

1. Gore Vidal, *Comment* (July 20, 1955).

2. Paul Smolarcik, "How Americans Watch TV," *A&E Monthly* (November, 1994), p. 6.

3. Dan Rather, "Donahue," (December 1, 1994).

4. "Declining Standards in News: Is It All Television's Fault?," Alfred I. duPont Forum, Columbia University, Columbia University Graduate School of Journalism (January 27, 1994), p. 55.

5. Ibid. p. 28.

6. John D. Stevens, *Sensationalism and the New York Press* (New York: Columbia University Press, 1991), pp. 5–6.

7. John L. Hulteng, *The Messenger's Motives: Ethical Problems of the News Media*, Second Edition (Englewood Cliffs, N.J.: Prentice-Hall, Inc., 1985), p. 154.

8. Stevens, p. 78.

9. Hulteng, p. 18.

10. Herbert J. Gans, *Deciding What's News: A Study of* CBS Evening News, NBC Nightly News, Newsweek, *and* Time (New York: Pantheon Books, 1979).

11. Hulteng, p. 123.

12. Edward Bliss, Jr., *Now the News: The Story of Broadcast Journalism* (New York: Columbia University Press, 1991), p. 1.

13. Stevens, pp. 7–9.

14. Stephen Bates, *If No News, Send Rumors: Anecdotes of American Journalism* (New York: St. Martin's Press, 1985), p. 212.

15. Stevens, p. 9.

16. Bliss, Jr., pp. 2–3.

17. Ibid. pp. 20–21.

18. Ibid. p. 34.

19. Bates, p. 241.

20. Bliss, Jr., p. 336.

21. Bates, p. 241.

22. Neil Postman and Steve Powers, *How to Watch TV News* (New York: Penguin Books, 1992), p. 50.

23. "Declining Standards in News: Is It All Television's Fault?," p. 14.

24. Mort Rosenblum, *Who Stole the News: Why We Can't Keep Up With What Happens in the World and What We Can Do About It* (New York: John Wiley & Sons, Inc., 1993), p. 4.

25. Bates, pp. 50–56, and Rosenblum, pp. 8–9.

Chapter 3

1. Thomas Jefferson, letter to James Curie, January 18, 1786.

2. Graham Knight, "Reality Effects: Tabloid Television News," *Queen's Quarterly*, vol. 96, no.1 (Spring, 1989), p. 94.

3. David Shaw, "Obsessed With Flash and Trash," *Los Angeles Times* (February 16, 1994), p. 1A.

4. S. Elizabeth Bird, *For Enquiring Minds: A Cultural Study of Supermarket Tabloids* (Knoxville, Tenn.: The University of Tennessee Press, 1992), p. 13.

5. Ibid. p. 16.

6. Ibid. p. 18.

7. Ibid. p. 21.

8. Ibid. p. 24.

9. Ibid. p. 207.

10. Edward Bliss, Jr., *Now The News: The Story of Broadcast Journalism* (New York: Columbia University Press, 1991), p. 288.

11. Marc Gunther, *The House That Roone Built* (Boston: Little, Brown and Company, 1994), p. 81.

12. Bliss, Jr., p. 295.

13. Larry Reibstein, "Trash + Class = Cash: The Battle of the TV News Magazine Shows," *Newsweek* (April 11, 1994), p. 64.

14. Howard Kurtz, "Sex! Mayhem! 'Now'! In the Newsmagazine Derby, NBC's Star-Driven Vehicle Puts A Sheen on Sensationalism," *The Washington Post* (March 14, 1994), p. D1.

15. Reibstein, p. 64.

16. Krista Bradford, "The Big Sleaze," *Rolling Stone* (February 18, 1993), pp. 39–43, 69.

17. Mike Tharp and Betsy Streisand, "Tabloid TV's Blood Lust," *U.S. News & World Report* (July 25, 1994), pp. 47–48.

18. Richard Zoglin, "Manson Family Values," *Time* (March 21, 1994), p. 77.

19. Neil Postman and Steve Powers, *How to Watch TV News* (New York: Penguin Books, 1992), p. 93.

20. Tim Funk, "'Inside Edition' anchor," *The Charlotte Observer* (September 20, 1994), p. 2E.

21. Tharp and Streisand, p. 48.

22. Telephone interview with Steve Rendall (January 13, 1995).

23. Richard Zoglin, "Easing the Sleaze," *Time* (December 6, 1993), pp. 72–74.

24. Dennis McDougal, "Donahue's Dilemma: Balancing Truth, Trash," *The Los Angeles Times* (January 28, 1990), Calendar, p. 8.

25. Knight, p. 106.

26. Stephen Bates, *If No News, Send Rumors: Anecdotes of American Journalism* (New York: St. Martin's Press, 1985), p. 183.

27. H. Eugene Goodwin, *Groping for Ethics in Journalism* (Ames, Iowa: Iowa State University Press, 1983), p. 192.

28. Bradford, pp. 42–43.

29. Tharp and Streisand, p. 48.

30. Shaw, p. 1A.

31. Ibid.

32. Ibid.

Chapter 4

1. David Frost, attributed, CBS Television, 1971.

2. Patricia Joyner Priest and Joseph R. Dominick, "Pulp Pulpits: Self-Disclosure on 'Donahue,'" *Journal of Communication*, vol. 44, no. 4 (Autumn, 1994), pp. 82–83.

3. Vicki Abt and Mel Seesholtz, "The Shameless World of Phil, Sally and Oprah: Television Talk Shows and the Deconstructing of Society," *Journal of Popular Culture*, vol. 28, no. 1 (Summer, 1994), p. 202.

4. Elayne Rapping, "Daytime Inquiries," *The Progressive* (October, 1991), pp. 36–38.

5. Rolonda Watts, publicity materials, 1995.

6. Abt and Seesholtz, p. 208.

7. Telephone interview with Steve Rendall (January 13, 1995).

8. Rapping, pp. 37–38.

9. Rolonda Watts, publicity materials, 1995.

10. Deborah Prothrow-Stith, M.D., with Michaele Weissman, *Deadly Consequences* (New York: HarperCollins Publishers, 1991), p. 32.

11. Joshua Meyrowitz, *No Sense of Place: The Impact of Electronic Media on Social Behavior* (New York: Oxford University Press, 1985), p. 14.

12. Abt and Seesholtz, p. 198.

13. Tom Shales, "We're Mad As Hell. . . . At Daytime TV, Getting Sleazier By the Minute," *The Washington Post* (March 19, 1995), p. G1.

14. Dennis McDougal, "Donahue's Dilemma: Balancing Truth, Trash," *The Los Angeles Times* (January 28, 1990), Calendar, p. 8.

15. Lawrence W. Lichty and Douglas Gomery, "More is Less," in *The Future of News: Television-Newspapers-Wire Services-Newsmagazines*, eds. Philip S. Cook, Douglas Gomery, and Lawrence W. Lichty (Washington, D.C.: The Woodrow Wilson Center Press, 1992), p. 4.

Chapter 5

1. Stephen Bates, *If No News, Send Rumors: Anecdotes of American Journalism* (New York: St. Martin's Press, 1985), p. 67.

2. Meg Greenfield, "In Defense of Sensationalism: The Media and the O.J. Simpson Case," *Newsweek* (September 26, 1994), p. 72.

3. Dan Rather, "Donahue" (December 1, 1994).

4. Deborah Baldwin, "Is It Fact? Or Is It Fiction?," *Common Cause Magazine* (Winter, 1993), p. 27.

5. Telephone interview with Steve Rendall (January 13, 1995).

6. "Declining Standards in News: Is It All Television's Fault?," Alfred I. duPont Forum, Columbia University, Columbia University Graduate School of Journalism (January 27, 1994), p. 21.

7. Ibid. p. 35.

8. Bates, p. 129.

9. Ibid. p. 8.

10. Ibid. p. 70.

11. Jung S. Ryu, "Public Affairs and Sensationalism in Local TV News Programs," *Journalism Quarterly*, vol. 59, no. 1 (Spring, 1982), p. 74.

12. Ibid. p. 78.

13. Howard Kurtz, "MURDER! MAYHEM! RATINGS! Tabloid Sensationalism Is Thriving on TV News," *The Washington Post* (July 4, 1993), p. A1.

14. "Declining Standards in News: Is It All Television's Fault?," p. 54.

15. Barbara Bliss Osborn, "If It Bleeds, It Leads. . . . If It Votes, It Don't: A Survey of L.A.'s Local 'News' Shows," *EXTRA!* (September/October, 1994), p. 15.

16. Deborah Prothrow-Stith, M.D., with Michaele Weissman, *Deadly Consequences* (New York: HarperCollins Publishers, 1991), p. 46.

17. Kurtz, p. A1.

18. Prothrow-Stith, M.D., with Weissman, p. 33.

19. Rick Marin and Peter Katel, "Miami's Crime Time Live," *Newsweek* (June 20, 1994), pp. 71–72.

20. Andy Meisler, "Blunting TV News's Sharp Edges," *The New York Times National* (December 14, 1994), p. D20.

21. Elizabeth Kolbert, "Television Gets Closer Look As a Factor in Real Violence," *The New York Times National* (December 14, 1994), pp. A1, D20.

Chapter 6

1. Dan Nimmo and James E. Combs, *Nightly Horrors: Crisis Coverage by Television Network News* (Knoxville, Tenn.: The University of Tennessee Press, 1985), p. 198.

2. Edward Bliss, Jr., *Now The News: The Story of Broadcast Journalism* (New York: Columbia University Press, 1991), p. 37.

3. Erica Goode and Katia Hetter, "The Selling of Reality," *U.S. News & World Report* (July 25, 1994), p. 54.

4. Larry Reibstein, "Trash + Class = Cash: The Battle of the TV News Magazine Shows," *Newsweek* (April 11, 1994), p. 64.

5. Mike Tharp and Betsy Streisand, "Tabloid TV's Blood Lust," *U.S. News & World Report* (July 25, 1994), pp. 47–48.

6. "Declining Standards in News: Is It All Television's Fault?," Alfred I. duPont Forum, Columbia University, Columbia University Graduate School of Journalism (January 27, 1994), p. 13.

7. Richard Zoglin, "The Cops and the Cameras," *Time* (April 6, 1992), p. 62.

8. Goode and Hetter, p. 54.

9. Joe Saltzman, "'Reality': Propaganda of the Worst Kind," *USA Today Magazine* (January, 1992), p. 93.

10. Telephone interview with Steve Rendall (January 13, 1995).

11. Zoglin, p. 63.

12. "A Warrantless Camera Crew," *Newsweek* (September 26, 1994), p. 70.

13. John L. Hulteng, *The Messenger's Motives: Ethical Problems of the News Media*, Second Edition (Englewood Cliffs, N.J.: Prentice-Hall, Inc., 1985), p. 154.

14. Goode and Hetter, p. 51.

15. Deborah Prothrow-Stith, M.D., with Michaele Weissman, *Deadly Consequences* (New York: HarperCollins Publishers, 1991), p. 34.

16. Goode and Hetter, p. 51.

17. Angela Wright, "Charlotte Viewer Helps Collar Murder Suspect," *The Charlotte Observer* (January 9, 1995), pp. 1A, 4A.

18. Joe Flint, "Reality Shows: Cop Trend Unabated in New Rosters," *Variety* (January 9–15, 1995), pp. 51, 55.

19. Joe Flint, "A Ghost of a Chance: Paranormal Fare Set to Battle an Expanded Police Force," *Variety* (January 9–15, 1995), pp. 51, 54, 56.

Chapter 7

1. David Shaw, "Obsessed With Flash and Trash," *The Los Angeles Times* (February 16, 1994), p. 1A.

2. H. Eugene Goodwin, *Groping for Ethics in Journalism* (Ames, Iowa: Iowa State University Press, 1983), pp. 10–14.

3. John L. Hulteng, *The Messenger's Motives: Ethical Problems of the News Media*, Second Edition (Englewood Cliffs, N.J.: Prentice-Hall, Inc., 1985), pp. 63–64.

4. Shaw, p. 1A.

5. Ibid.

6. Goodwin, pp. 247–248.

7. Hulteng, pp. 63–64.

8. Susanne Roschwalb, "Does Television Belong in the Courtroom?," *USA Today Magazine* (November, 1994), pp. 69–70.

9. Krista Bradford, "The Big Sleaze," *Rolling Stone* (February 18, 1993), p. 69.

10. Colman McCarthy, "'Between You and Me,'" *The Charlotte Observer* (January 7, 1995), p. 13A.

11. Hulteng, p. 83.

12. McCarthy, p. 13A.

13. Ibid.

14. Ibid.

15. Claude Lewis, "Painting a Black Face on Crime," *The Charlotte Observer* (November 4, 1994), p. 13A.

16. John McCormick, "Why Parents Kill," *Newsweek* (November 14, 1994), pp. 31–34.

17. Deborah Prothrow-Stith, M.D., with Michaele Weissman, *Deadly Consequences* (New York: HarperCollins Publishers, 1991), p. 177.

18. Jerry Adler, Ginny Carroll, Vern Smith, and Patrick Rogers, "Innocents Lost," *Newsweek* (November 14, 1994), pp. 26–30.

19. Gregory Freeman, "Television Can Change The Channel On Hispanic Roles," *CRISIS* (October, 1994), p. 5.

20. Marty Baumann, "Racial, Ethnic Groups Give Mixed Reviews to Media," *USA Today* (July 26, 1994), p. 2A.

21. Howard Kurtz, "MURDER! MAYHEM! RATINGS! Tabloid Sensationalism Is Thriving on TV News," *The Washington Post* (July 4, 1993), p. A1.

22. Bradford, p. 69.

23. David Bianculli and Gail Shister, "How TV Covered the Dwyer Suicide," *The Phildadelphia Inquirer* (January 23, 1987), p. D1.

24. Hulteng, pp. 57–58.

25. Deborah Baldwin, "Is It Fact? Or Is It Fiction?," *Common Cause Magazine* (Winter, 1993), pp. 25–29.

26. John Schwartz, Frank Washington, Charles Fleming, and Kendall Hamilton, "No Scandal, No Story," *Newsweek* (February 22, 1993), pp. 42–43.

27. "Declining Standards in News: Is It All Television's Fault?," Alfred I. duPont Forum, Columbia University, Columbia University Graduate School of Journalism (January 27, 1994), p. 30.

28. Telephone interview with Steve Rendall (January 13, 1995).

29. Glenn G. Sparks, Tricia Hansen, and Rani Shah, "Do Televised Depictions of Paranormal Events Influence Viewers' Beliefs?," *Skeptical Inquirer*, vol. 18 (Summer, 1994), pp. 386–395.

Chapter 8

1. Stephen Bates, *If No News, Send Rumors: Anecdotes of American Journalism* (New York: St. Martin's Press, 1985), p. 18.

2. Telephone interview with Tom Colbert (October 10, 1994).

3. Tom Dworetzky, "Teens: Will TV Become Their Virtual (and only) Reality?," *OMNI*, vol. 14 (September, 1992), p. 16.

4. "Declining Standards in News: Is It All Television's Fault?," Alfred I. duPont Forum, Columbia University, Columbia University Graduate School of Journalism (January 27, 1994), p. 33.

5. Carl Bernstein, "The Idiot Culture," *The New Republic* (June 8, 1992), pp. 22–26.

6. Ibid.

7. Ibid.

8. Neil Postman and Steve Powers, *How to Watch TV News* (New York: Penguin Books, 1992), p. 52.

9. David Shaw, "Obsessed With Flash and Trash," *Los Angeles Times* (February 16, 1994), p. 1A.

10. David Lieberman, "Rivals Have Descended on Tabloids: More Players Make it Hard to Pitch to Inquiring Minds," *USA Today* (August 9, 1994), pp. B1, B2.

11. Ibid. p. B2.

12. "Declining Standards in News: Is It All Television's Fault?," p. 17.

13. Telephone interview with Steve Rendall (January 13, 1995).

14. "Declining Standards in News: Is It All Television's Fault?," p. 64.

Index